Long Melford through the ages
A guide to the buildings and streets

by Barry L. Wall

Photographs by Ken Haines

EAST ANGLIAN MAGAZINE LTD IPSWICH SUFFOLK

For Gaynor and Lori and all others who
enjoy exploring Suffolk as we do.

Printed & Published by
East Anglian Magazine Ltd.,
6 Great Colman Street,
Ipswich, Suffolk
© *Barry L. Wall 1986*

I.S.B.N. 0 900227 78 8

LIST OF ILLUSTRATIONS

	Page
Kentwell Hall	13
Long Melford Church: Engraving by J.P. Neale	17
Melford Hall: J.P. Neale's engraving of c. 1825	18
Holy Trinity Church	28
The Lady Chapel	28
The Martyn Chapel	29
The church from the North East	29
The original Lady Chapel	32
The East window of the Chantry Chapel	32
The porch c. 1481	35
North aisle: Adoration of the Magi c. 1350	35
The Clopton chantry chapel	36
Clopton's tomb	36
Sir William Cordell's Tomb c. 1582	37
The Lady Chapel	38
The Lady Chapel: The arch braced tie-beam roof	43
The Lady Chapel: Niches and blank tracery	43
Kentwell Hall: The Moat House	47
Kentwell Hall: Interior of the Great Hall of Lutons	49
Kentwell Hall: South front	55
Kentwell Hall: Porch and great bay of the hall by John Clopton c. 1470	55
Kentwell Hall: East wing from the Cedar Lawn	56
Kentwell Hall: East Turret	56
Kentwell Hall: North front	57
Kentwell Hall: Hopper's Screen and dado of c. 1823	57
Kentwell Hall: Garden delights, the gazebo and bridge	59
Kentwell Hall: The seventeenth century Dovehouse	59
Melford Hall: West front	63
Melford Hall: East front	63

Melford Hall: Outline plan showing Abbot Reeve's Hall 65
Melford Hall: Thorp's plan of c. 1615 66
Melford Hall: N.E. Turret 67
Melford Hall: Cordell's Porch of c. 1550 67
Melford Hall: West Front as altered by Hopper in 1813-15 70
Melford Hall: The Grand Staircase by Hopper..................73
A colonnade supporting the curved and coffered ceiling 73
Melford Hall: The Garden House or Gazebo 74
Melford Hall: The Garden House 74
Melford Place: The home of the Martyn family................81
Melford Place: Interior of the chapel........................81
Melford Place: The Chapel roof 85
Melford Place: The Chapel Seventeenth century gallery at the West end..85
Melford Place: The Chapel. Some of the Renaissance panels 87
Two of the houses flanking the Green 89
Gateways on The Green: The restored entrance to Cordell's almshouses..91
Gateways on The Green: The entrance gateway to Melford Hall 92
The Hospital of the Holy and undivided Trinity 93
Melford Green: Late 17C row of modest cottages 94
Late 18C reminiscent of a doll's house......................94
Melford Green: Two more hybrid houses....................95
Little Green: Timber-frame and plaster house.................98
Little Green: An early 19C grey brick terrace 98
Two views from the footpath by the Mill. The Mill ford which gave the village its name. A fine display of topiary on the banks of the moat......................................99
Brook House 101
The Bull Hotel 102
Hall Street, East Side: Nos. 7,8 and 9 105
Hall Street, East Side: Blyth House........................105
Hall Street, East Side: Tudor Cottages c. 1550 108

Hall Street, East Side: Chestnut House 108
Hall Street, East Side: Lime Cottage 109
Hall Street, East Side: Mansell Hall....................... 111
Hall Street, East Side: Archway Cottage 111
Hall Street, East Side: Corpus Christi or Cadge's House.......... 112
Hall Street, East Side: Forge Cottage...................... 115
Hall Street, West Side: Georgian bays fronting older cottages.
All very typical of Melford 115
Hall Street, Chapel Green: Medieval chimneys betray the
origins of this apparently Victorian house 116
Hall Street, West Side: The Old House..................... 119
Hall Street, West Side: Late Georgian facade c. 1815 to
Foundry House on the left and an earlier stuccoed front
to the Cock and Bell 120
Hall Street, West Side: Hanwell House..................... 123
Hall Street, West Side: List House........................ 123
Westgate Street: Early 19C elegance, 1835—38 125
Westgate Street: Late 16C timber, plastered a century later....... 125
Westgate House, 18C elegance again 126
Bull Lane: Two timber-framed houses...................... 127
Bull Lane: Another Timber-framed house 128
Bridge Street Farm: A Hall house......................... 129
Bridge Street, Ford Hall 129

Long Melford Church

INTRODUCTION

Long Melford is a large village, although some would say a small town, with a population of about 4,000. To the casual visitor there are no signs of a major industry but on the banks of the river Stour, a short distance from the village centre, is a large and well-established manufacturing chemists. The river serves as a boundary between Suffolk and Essex and flows through some of England's loveliest countryside, a gentle and intimate landscape made famous by Constable and Gainsborough. Melford is one of a long chain of medieval cloth centres which includes Stoke-by-Nayland, Nayland, Bures, Sudbury, Cavendish and Clare, all of them in Suffolk and now subject to the pressures of the tourist industry. They cope with it remarkably well, especially Melford which has a good deal to offer the visitor. Apart from a unique and impressive collection of historic buildings, there are numerous antique shops and eating places, and a delightful nature reserve on the border with Sudbury which has picnic facilities and fishing.

There are several things about Melford that are unusual and set it apart from its neighbours and the first is indeed the length of the main thoroughfare. From Rodbridge Corner to High Street Farm is a distance of over three miles and it claims to be the longest village street in England. Suffolk is a county famous for beautiful medieval churches but Melford has one of national importance. It is built on a large scale but possesses an intimacy rarely found in great churches. There are two impressive Tudor mansions, one of them largely contemporary with Wolsey's Hampton Court, the other begun even earlier. Both have red brick walls and pepper-pot turrets reflected in their moats.

What makes the major buildings of Melford memorable to the most casual observer is their setting which has Melford Green as the focal point. It forms a huge triangle sloping down from north to south with the silvery grey mass of the church at the top partly obscured by another Tudor foundation, the Hospital of the Undivided Trinity, a group of almshouses built around a central court. The fine Renaissance turrets of Melford Hall soar above a red brick garden wall at the foot of the Green on the east side, while opposite a run of later houses cascades down towards the pretty little Victorian school.

Kentwell Hall lies behind the church and is just visible

from the churchyard but to reach it one must go down an avenue of limes almost a mile long. The full width and beauty of the house is only revealed as the avenue comes to an end. It has a romantic setting with moated gardens and parkland stretching away into the distance.

That any village should be so richly endowed is remarkable enough but there is more. From the foot of the Green, over the eighteenth century bridge which spans the Chad Brook — a tributary of the Stour, stretches the main street. It is broad and partly tree-lined with a mile of houses ranging from the fifteenth to the nineteenth centuries. New development, where it occurs, runs parallel on the east side and is, by and large, unobtrusive.

From the evidence of the buildings we can deduce that during the fifteenth century there was a high prosperity which continued through the Tudor dynasty. There are enough Georgian facades along Hall Street to show that it continued down the centuries in one form or another but it became spasmodic. By studying the village the history of England unfolds and it begins before the Romans came for beneath the village is another, almost forgotten, shrouded in mystery and without a name.

When I started on this work I was told more than once that there was nothing new to be written about Melford. It had all been done before. Well, that depends on the type of book one is looking for. This is not intended as a History of Melford because that has already been written by Sir William Parker in the late nineteenth century. It can rarely be purchased and copies are at a premium but they can be found in the reference libraries at Bury, Ipswich and Colchester. I have drawn on this source for much of the information about the early history of the manor of Melford Hall but apart from one quotation, which is acknowledged in the text, I found nothing in that great work to assist me when unraveling the complicated structural history of the house itself.

This book is about the buildings of Melford and the part they played in the story of the village; how they came to be built and when. Much of what has been written on the subject I found to be woefully inadequate and often incorrect which is astounding for such a famous village. The only answer was to start from scratch and reassess the buildings with a completely open mind and then compare my findings with what had already been written. As a result, Melford has proved to be a more exciting place than I thought possible and much new information has emerged. It is possible that some will not agree with my conclusions and I know I have left myself wide open to criticism by attacking cherished beliefs but that is what writing about history is all about. I have been as thorough with my research as possible but when there are no written records one is left with comparative study, observation and deduction. Only when I was certain that I had reached the right conclusions did I put pen to paper. I hope this book will prove to the reader that Melford is indeed a village of which not only Suffolk but England can be proud.

A SUMMARY OF THE HISTORY OF MELFORD

The Belgae were the first settled inhabitants. They arrived in England round about 100 B.C. from Germany. We know they were at Melford because fragments of their pottery and other artifacts have been found. Their settlement straddled both sides of Liston Lane where they lived in primitive huts, hunted, and fished from the nearby river. They owned herds of cattle, wove coarse cloth and led a relatively peaceful life. Their peace was to be disturbed with the arrival of the Romans under the Emperor Claudius in 43 A.D.

In order to colonise this country effectively the Romans set up a network of roads, three of which converged on Melford.

1) The London–Braintree road which linked with the Peddars Way at Ixworth. This can still be traced along the modern highway through Braintree but vanishes at a point this side of Gosfield Bridge. Thereafter fragments appear as hedgerows and footpaths and it passes close to the Romano-British settlement at Gestingthorpe before re-emerging just north of Rodbridge where it enters Melford as the main thoroughfare. It passes a little to the east of Hall Street at one point but crosses the ford at the foot of the Green and carries on towards Bury.

2) The road from Barham in Suffolk to Wixoe in Essex where it joins the VIA DEVANA (Colchester to Cambridge). At Melford it crosses the top of the Green and follows the present road to Clare.

3) A road thought to run from Colchester via Nayland of which only fragments have survived. A stretch appears at Newton Lays on the other side of Sudbury and runs to Great Waldingfield. It passes through Acton and joined road (2) at a point near Basset's Farm.

It would be very surprising if there were to be no traces of Romano-British occupation at such an important junction. Scattered archeological finds indicate that a substantial settlement existed along the west or left hand side of the main street going towards the Green. The most interesting discovery so far has been the villa or homestead off Liston Lane in the grounds of Melford Place in 1958. The finds included part of a tessellated pavement or floor of white limestone and red tile. There were some wall fragments and traces of other floors beneath which were found some Belgic pottery sherds. Elsewhere in the village finds have included more floor fragments, coins of the first and second centuries A.D., pottery of the same period and traces of burials. Sir William Parker in his HISTORY OF LONG MELFORD refers to finds at Stoneylands, again of Liston Lane, in 1828 while a pottery flask and other glass fragments were found behind The Old House in the 1960s. There must be a great deal more beneath houses of a later date still to be discovered.

SAXONS AND NORMANS

Unlike Sudbury, where the development of the town can be traced throughout the Saxon period, at Melford we are left with a gap of several centuries before the next significant event is recorded, with the presentation of the Manor to the Abbey of St. Edmundsbury. This occurred at some time between 1045 and 1065. The Manor had become the property of Queen Emma, the mother of Edward The Confessor, and was held in trust for her by Earl Alfric. The gift is confirmed by the Doomsday record and gives details of how prosperous the Manor was. In modern terms it extended to 1440 acres and as the description is the very first we have of the early medieval village it is worth listing some of the details.

   50 Acres of meadow and woodland for depasturing 60 hogs
   40 Villeins
   16 Serfs
   10 Bordari (Cottagers with a portion of land)
   30 Plough oxen
 300 Sheep
 140 Pigs
   12 Hives of Bees
   40 Husbandry Horses
    2 Water Mills
    2 Socmen holding 80 acres
    6 Ploughs of the Manor
   13 Ploughs belonging to the homagers

Such were the possessions of the Manor some twenty or so years after the original gift. This was just one of the manors owned by the Abbey in West Suffolk.

Another interesting fact emerges from the same source. We learn that the church had a manor of its own comprising some 240 acres, 18 furlongs in length and 1½ miles in breadth, later to become known as Monk's Manor. Why the church was so endowed is a mystery and it opens up the question of whether it was a minster church serving a much wider area as at St. Gregory's in Sudbury. In 1184 two thirds of the church's property was given to St. Saviour's Hospital at Bury by the great Abbot Sampson.

A third manor is mentioned in Doomsday as Kanewella, known to us now as Kentwell. It was a part of Melford outside the jurisdiction of the Abbey which was no bad thing in the light of later events.

The early village begins to take shape with three distinct settlements. The Hall with its mill at the foot of the Green by the ford which gave the village the name Millford. Another clustered around the church at the top of the Green, and a third more scattered in Kentwell Park.

Moving forward to 1214 we find King John passing through Melford on his way to Bury Abbey. It is possible, but by no means certain, that he spent a night at the Hall as guest of the Abbot, for on the fourth of November he granted the village a weekly market and an annual fair. Through this valuable gift we learn that the village was already spreading towards Sudbury because the market was held, not on the Green as one would expect, but almost a mile away on what is now Chapel Green. It has been suggested that the population at this time was around 600. Many of them were employed on the Manor but already the Abbey was leasing land out to merchants, tradesmen etc. while others were becoming involved in the wool trade.

They lived in simple constructions of timber, mud and thatch and the Hall was constructed from the same materials. The church, a more modest structure than today's was probably the only building of flint and stone. Nothing has survived from this era due to the great prosperity still to come through the wool and subsequent cloth trade of the fifteenth century.

The 1300s started well enough with more tenants paying rents for their land instead of service. Then in 1348-9 the horrendous Black Death swept across Europe almost halving the population. In East Anglia some villages, such as Little Cornard, were almost wiped out. Naturally Melford did not escape and the subsequent death toll caused a scarcity of labour and those who survived were to benefit. The Abbey of St. Edmundsbury having large estates covering most of West Suffolk, was obliged to lease out more of its land at cheaper rents. It was no longer prudent to insist that villeins should perform their compulsory free service when they could easily move on to a neighbouring manor, such as Kentwell, where they would be paid for the same work. From their wages many of them saved enough to buy a sheep or two of their own and from the sale of the wool could eventually earn enough to purchase their freedom legitimately. All tenants were still obliged to pay tithes to the Abbey, that was the law and the Abbot saw that it was obeyed.

The feudal system was beginning to crack and its demise was hastened with the Peasants' Revolt of 1381. The villeins had been banding together for years to oppose their lords and the system, and they were angry at the increasing wealth of the church and, of course, its power. John Ball had been preaching up and down the country about freedom and justice in the sight of God and so had the Friars from Sudbury as they toured the neighbouring villages. Parliament had brought in statutes to control and restrict the labourers' wages and the last straw was the imposition of the hated poll tax of fourpence per head. When the revolt came Melford was in the thick of it but, amazingly, in spite of being a monastic manor, no damage or looting is recorded.

The local ringleaders were John Wrawe and Geoffrey Parfrey, both from Sudbury. Wrawe had been to London and had met up with the Kent rebel leaders and was to return to Sudbury to lead the Suffolk rebellion. He led a mob to nearby Liston where they sacked and wrecked the home of the notorious moneylender Richard Lyons. They then moved on to Cavendish in search of Chief Justice Cavendish who was responsible for enforcing the Statute of Labourers in East Anglia. They found he had fled but hearing that his treasures were stored in the church tower for safety they demanded entry and carried them off. They then made their way to Melford, not to pillage, which considering the connection with Bury Abbey was remarkable, but for refreshment at a tavern on the Green owned by a man called Onewene. They paid him 3/4d for their victuals before moving on to Bury where the Prior at the Abbey was murdered by his own serfs. Justice Cavendish was run to ground at Lakenheath where his head was struck off and carried to Bury for display. After the rebellion came retribution and a brief return to serfdom doomed to failure. Things were never quite the same again. By the end of the century the Manor of Melford was still owned by the Abbey but the inhabitants were free men renting their houses and lands and sometimes purchasing them outright. The church was rebuilt on a larger scale, though not so large as the present structure. Social life was expanded by the founding of no less than six religious guilds. Houses were more sturdily constructed, still timber-framed but thatch was already giving way to small tiles. Melford was entering its period of high prosperity.

PROSPERITY AND THE REFORMATION

The symbol of the great wealth which the cloth trade brought to Melford is of course the church. To understand how such a noble building came about we need to take a look at a part of the village not under the jurisdiction of the Abbey. In 1373 the manor of Lutons (now Kentwell) had become the property of Katherine Mylde who nine years later married Thomas Clopton. Although the marriage lasted just over one year she managed to bear him a son and so began the long line of Cloptons of Kentwell. Katherine was left a widow and very soon remarried to Sir William Tendring of Stoke-by-Nayland.

Her son William grew up to be a fine soldier and eventually took over the manor on his mother's death. Before he died in 1446 he had built for his family a very noble chapel flanking the chancel of the church; this is now known as the Kentwell aisle. When he died his tomb, with his effigy in armour upon it, was placed in the chapel. He was succeeded by his son John who was twenty three when he inherited the estate which he was to hold for fifty one years. He was a close friend and neighbour of the Earl of Oxford whose castle was at Hedingham and who was also Lord of the Manor of Lavenham. This friendship was to land Clopton in deep trouble for in 1461 they were both arrested with Oxford's son Aubrey De Vere, Sir Thomas Tuddenham, Sir John Montgomery and William Tyrell. They were charged with corresponding with the exiled Queen Margaret of Anjou, which counted as treason and for which they were imprisoned in the Tower of London. Both Oxford and his son were executed but Clopton was released and allowed to return home to Kentwell. Very soon after that a new north aisle, a continuation of the Kentwell aisle, was constructed on ambitious lines and it would be quite reasonable to suggest that this was done as a thank offering for his life being spared.

There can be no doubt that the new work on the north side of the church inspired the great rebuilding scheme of the nave, chancel, south aisle and Martyn chapel. The inscriptions on the walls and the many wills of the period show that John Clopton was the organiser, fund raiser and chief benefactor. There is one glaring omission from the list of subscribers, the Abbot of Bury, head of one of the richest monastries in England and Lord of the Manor of Melford.

While the Cloptons were establishing themselves at Kentwell another prominent family had set up home at the other end of the village. Roger Martyn from Dorset was the first to settle at Melford Place and he died in 1438 succeeded by his son Lawrence who in turn died the year before Clopton's arrest. He left three sons, Richard, Lawrence and Roger. Roger was a Bencher at Lincoln's Inn and was offered a position as Secretary of State which he refused. The Martyns had built themselves a chapel on the south side of the chancel of the old church and when the great rebuilding scheme got under way they rebuilt it to blend in with the new work. They were reluctant to destroy the windows from the previous chapel so they were re-used, a regrettable act of economy which has spoiled the rhythm of the south side. They also subscribed towards the cost of other parts of the church. Their house, a large timber-framed hall house with brick embellishments, stood opposite the Old Market Place, now Chapel Green. The Green takes its name from the chapel of St. James which stood there and was watched over and often maintained by the Martyns. It is first heard of in the will of Roger Carter in 1464 and appears in various wills after then in 1479, 1535, and 1538. It is shown on an estate map of 1580 but by 1613 it had become a secular building and no more is heard of it after 1615.

Between Melford Place and The Green at the other end of the village runs Hall Street. Along this important thoroughfare several hall-type houses of timber were erected by the clothiers and wealthy tradesmen. Most of them had a central hall, often single storied, flanked by one, or usually two, crosswings. Several of them have survived though often subdivided and refronted. In one of them probably lived John Cordell, the son of a merchant from Edmonton in Middlesex. He had a very talented son named William who took up law as a career and rose to great heights. We shall hear more of him later. The fifteenth century was drawing to a close with England curiously unaffected by the great Renaissance movement which had transformed art and architecture in Italy and France for decades. But not for long; the new century was to be one of great change not only for the arts but for religion and politics.

In 1496 John Clopton saw his church completed but died the following year leaving the famous Lady Chapel unfinished. He was buried close to the high alter, the most prestigious position in the church. His son William, aged forty seven, inherited his estate. By this time the market had moved on to the Great Green where was erected a market cross of which only the base has survived. A smaller market operated opposite The Bull where a permanent shelter housed two or three stalls. Henry VII had been on the throne now for twelve years and had another twelve to go.

At Lavenham the Earl of Oxford and Thomas Spring were rebuilding their church, no doubt envious of Melford's achievement and determined to surpass it in some way. The Abbey at Bury still held sway over most of West Suffolk and by 1515 a Melford man, John Reeve, was elected Abbot. He rebuilt Melford Hall on a grand scale and in 1534 leased it out to Dame Frances Pennington for a period of thirty years with the proviso that one of the best chambers should be made available to him for the annual Manorial Court. Five years later disaster came to

Long Melford Church: Engraving by J.P. Neale showing the Georgian brick tower 1825. Note the one remaining pinnacle on the clerestory. In 1825 some of the windows were bricked up but the artist has not shown this.

Melford Hall: J.P. Neale's engraving of c. 1825

him and there was a great upheaval in the affairs of Melford.

In 1539 the great abbeys were dissolved by Henry VIII and all their lands were surrendered to the Crown, including the Manor of Melford. Dame Frances was allowed to remain as tenant but her rent was henceforth to be paid into the Royal Exchequer, the other tenants were obliged to do the same. Meanwhile the young lawyer William Cordell had risen to great heights in his career and was showing great interest in Melford Hall. In the last year of the king's reign, in 1547, he was granted the entire manor for an annual rent of £100. As for the Cloptons, a second William was now owner of Kentwell and he lost no time in taking advantage of the situation by securing those parts of Monk's Manor which his family had leased for generations. Cordell got the remainder. At Melford Place the Martyn family were entering their dark period which was to last well into the seventeenth century. They were devout Roman Catholics and were to suffer accordingly.

With the accession of Edward VI in 1547 England was now a Protestant country and within a few weeks came the order to remove all images whatsoever from the churches. Later in the same year came further orders for the preparation of inventories of all church goods. The inventory for Melford shows a church exceptionally well endowed especially with regard to plate which was what the Crown was after. It all had to be surrendered to the commissioners except for sufficient implements to conduct Divine Service, i.e. one chalice and one paten. Roger Martyn left a description of the eastern end of the church as it was before the Reformation and this has to be read to appreciate fully just how much has been lost. Priceless works of art were destroyed, disposed of and sometimes hidden. Sadly the church had only been completed fifty one years. Edward died young so when his sister Mary became Queen there was a brief return to Catholicism which meant the return of some of the furnishings but on her death they were removed once more.

In 1554 Mary confirmed the grant of the Manor of Melford to William Cordell and released him from the rent charge. This was in recognition of his "past good, true, faithful and acceptable service." Honours had been heaped on him by 1558, he was M.P. for Suffolk, knighted, and made Speaker for the House of Commons. He was to become Solicitor General and Master of the Rolls. When Elizabeth became Queen he was to serve her as faithfully as he had her father and her brother and sister. He was of course ambitious, he would never have succeeded so well otherwise, but he was also kind and shrewd.

Melford Hall had already been substantially rebuilt by the last Abbot of Bury and few alterations were necessary to make it one of the finest Tudor houses in East Anglia. In 1578 Cordell was host to Elizabeth who was on one of her famous 'progresses'. Thomas Churchyard has left a much quoted description of her arrival at the Suffolk border and I make no excuses for including part of it here:

> "There were 200 young gentlemen cladde all in white velvet and 300 of the graver sort apparrelled in black velvet coates with faire chains . . . with 1500 servying men all on horseback well and bravelie mounted, to receive the Queens Hignesse into Suffolke . . . and there was such sumptuous feastings and bankets as seldom seen before, The Maister of the Rolles, Sir William Cordell, was the first that beganne this great feastinge at his house at Melforde, and did light such a candle to the rest of the shire, that they were glad bountifullie and franklie to followe the same example . . ."

Five years previously Cordell had built the Hospital in front of the Church on land formerly belonging to Monk's Manor. Just three years after entertaining his Queen he died and was buried beneath a sumptuous tomb in the chancel of the church. He left a widow but no issue so after Lady Cordell's death the estate passed to his sister Lady Alington and thence to the Savage family. When Elizabeth visited Melford much of what she saw still stands though somewhat altered. The Clopton's new mansion at Kentwell had been finished about 1563 and although William Clopton was no doubt invited by his neighbour to meet the Queen there is no record of her visiting his new house. Melford Hall has changed considerably since her visit but Kentwell has retained its exterior almost down to the last brick.

Throughout Elizabeth's reign the church was systematically stripped of its wall paintings and much of the stained glass. The walls were whitewashed leaving the interior cold and bare. It was to suffer more during the next century and the deterioration would continue until the much maligned Victorians put a stop to it.

THE SEVENTEENTH CENTURY AND AFTER

The seventeenth century began disastrously in Melford with an outbreak of a virulent plague. It began in May 1604 with the death of fifteen people, a further fourteen died in June. It was a hot summer and the death toll soared in July and August when ninety two more deaths are recorded. It was probably a form of Bubonic plague carried by fleas and this particular outbreak seems to have been confined to Melford. It was most likely brought into the village by one of the travellers using the many taverns which now existed.

The Bull and The Hart stood almost opposite each other near the ford and still do. The Bull has become one of the foremost hotels in East Anglia and The Hart is now Brook House. By 1678 there were three others in Hall Street, The White Horse, The Fox, and The Bell. Three more lined the Green, The Black Lion, The Angel, and The Eight Bells. The last named had previously been called the White Lion and is now Falkland House. The taverns fulfilled an important role in the life of the village offering hospitality to visiting merchants and through-travellers to Bury or Norwich. They would certainly be packed to overflowing during the annual Whitsuntide fair which had become famous over the centuries and was to become more so as a Horse Fair in later years.

Throughout Elizabeth's reign the Anglican church had become firmly established in spite of attempted disruption by the Papists and the Puritans. Puritanism had started out as a doctrine imported from Geneva after Mary's death. It had taken root in East Anglia but was firmly kept in check by Elizabeth who was determined to strike a middle course. Neither was it tolerated by the first two Stuart monarchs. Because of this many from this area emigrated to the New World where they were guaranteed religious freedom. Those who chose to remain continued to work towards a religious revolution. It is ironic that these people regarded Latin inscriptions in churches as superstitious and yet they were the very people who encouraged the notorious witch hunts. During 1645–1647 some 200 'witches' were executed in East Anglia. One wonders what they thought of poor Rose Sheap of Melford who on the 26th April 1618 gave birth to a child with two faces, four arms and four legs according to the parish records. The term 'Siamese Twins' was not yet heard of.

At Melford Place the Martyn family were recusants and because of this, under a statute of Elizabeth, their movements were restricted to within five miles of their home. In 1627 Sir Roger Martyn was granted an exemption from this cruel law. He became an ardent Royalist and died in 1657.

Another ardent Royalist and Catholic was Lady Savage, widow of Viscount Savage, who had inherited Melford Hall on the death of her husband in 1635. In 1639 she became extremely wealthy when her father died leaving her Hengrave Hall near Bury and St. Osyth's Priory in Essex. Two years later she was created a Countess in her own right. Because of her religious and Royalist associations she came under attack at the outbreak of the Civil War. Her house at St. Osyth was invaded and sacked by a mob which caused her to flee to Melford. Unfortunately she was pursued and was obliged to move on to Bury and eventually London. Melford Hall was plundered by a mob estimated to be between two and three thousand strong. They left it a wreck and even carried off the deer in the park. Lady Savage, now Countess Rivers, ended her life in the Debtors' Prison in 1650. By the strange laws of coincidence her Melford property was mortgaged to Sir John Cordell, a relative of Sir William Cordell who had been granted the Manor in 1547. It was his task to repair the damage to the Hall and refurnish it.

The last male Clopton at Kentwell died in 1618 at the early age of twenty seven. His two sons had died in infancy so the estate passed to his daughter who at the young age of thirteen was married to Sir Simonds D'Ewes. In 1650 their daughter Cecilia and her husband Sir Thomas D'Arcy became the owners and did much to modernise the house's interior.

During the seventeenth century the cloth industry was coming to an end at Melford and the ordinary villagers were mostly employed at the great houses or on the land. There were of course many service industries such as shops and inns of which the former supplied goods not only for the gentry at Melford Hall and Kentwell but also the other great houses at Liston and Acton.

The peace of the village was disturbed in July 1648 when a political discussion at The Bull between Roger Grene and Richard Evered developed into violent argument resulting in Evered being knifed to death. Of Grene we know nothing but Evered is described as a 'substantial yeoman', however whether that refers to his bulk or his wealth is not clear. He was buried in the churchyard on the 26th July but what became of his assailant is apparently unrecorded.

At Melford Place, following the Restoration of Charles II, Roger Martyn was rewarded for his family's loyalty with the title of Baronet in 1677. Things did not go so well for the Rector, Dr. Bisbie, who was ejected from his post for not swearing allegiance to William of Orange in 1689. The nonconformists were becoming very strong in Suffolk and a group were already meeting in Melford as early as 1650, usually in someone's barn or kitchen. They eventually built themselves a chapel in Hall Street in 1712 which still stands.

The eighteenth century saw a great improvement in agriculture and the large estates flourished under careful management producing, among other things, huge quantities of barley for malting. The river Stour had been made navigable from Sudbury to Mistley and this made it possible to send all kinds of produce to the London markets by sea. Of manufacturing industries there was precious little though a small paper-making mill was established on the river. Bricklayers and carpenters were kept busy as can be seen by the many Georgian houses which line Hall Street, and major work was being carried out at Melford Hall by Sir Cordell Firebrace. Liston Hall and Acton Place, two impressive Palladian mansions, were also built during the century and it is a tragedy that they have not survived. In 1786 Melford Hall was sold for the last time, the purchaser Sir Harry Parker who came from Honington Hall in Warwickshire. He was a descendant of Margaret Hyde, heiress of Lord Chancellor Clarendon, and the two names have been linked since 1674. Sir Harry was the sixth Baronet, the title having come to the family in 1681.

Four years previously Kentwell Hall had been inherited by Richard Moore, a bachelor and a spendthrift. His family had purchased the Hall in 1706 and were respected in the county, two of them holding the office of High Sheriff of Suffolk. Richard Moore's life story is one of wasted opportunity and farcical decline, an ideal villain for the pages of Jane Austen or Thackeray and a terrible lesson and a warning to the more humble children of Melford. He was only thirteen when he came into his inheritance and in 1796 at the age of twenty seven he married Sidney Arabella Cotton. Their first born was a son named Willoughby and he was quickly followed by several others. The marriage seems to have been quite happy at first and the couple did much to improve their mansion in 1801. Richard began spending money like water and soon had a reputation as a gambler and a born loser. Not surprisingly his marriage began to crack up and in 1812 Long Melford and all Suffolk reeled under the shock of a scandalous divorce. It was granted him by Act of Parliament because of his wife's 'unlawful familiarity, criminal intercourse and adulterous conversation with John Miller, Steward of Kentwell.' Poor Sidney Arabella, as the guilty party, was doomed to oblivion while her ex-husband became High Sheriff of Suffolk.

Richard continued to gamble and his debts steadily mounted with the inevitable result that the estate became heavily mortgaged. The beautiful lime avenue was sold to Clementi, the piano maker and tree-felling began from the mansion end. Timber was a very valuable asset in those days and we must be eternally grateful to Richard's mother for buying back the trees from Clementi. In 1823 the house and contents were sold by auction but not enough was raised to cover his debts. He was declared bankrupt and ended his life in the Debtors' Prison three years later.

This sad story has brought us neatly into the nineteenth century, a time of expansion for Melford with the introduction of manufacturing industries. The most important event was the arrival of the railway in 1865 in the form of a single line track from the main line at Marks Tey to Haverhill with a branch line, also single track, via Lavenham to Bury St. Edmunds. The station was situated at the far end of the village towards Sudbury where numerous labourers' cottages were also being built. Close by the station was constructed a large Maltings.

In 1843 Messrs. Ward and Silver opened their Iron Foundry in Hall Street where they made agricultural implements, gates, railings and some domestic articles. During the century they expanded and moved to a new site across the road where they also opened a timber yard and workshop. By 1900 they were employing eighty men, including twelve blacksmiths, and they manufactured waggons, tumbrils, elevators, and harrows. The site covered some three and a half acres and it flourished for 110 years until closed down in 1953.

The cloth industry was virtually at an end although there were one or two silk weavers working on hand looms for Sudbury firms. The weavers' skills were not entirely wasted, at least as far as the men were concerned, because they were needed for the coconut mat making which was introduced into Melford round about 1860. The coconut fibre was prepared and twisted or 'spun' by the women but was heavy going when it came to the weaving so that part was done by men. The industry was dealt a blow when mat making was introduced into the prisons resulting in a reduction in wages. There was a prolonged strike in 1885 which caused much bad feeling and resentment which surfaced again in the General Election of that year.

The election was a straight contest between the Liberal candidate, Mr. Cuthbert Quilter of Hintlesham Hall and the Conservative Mr. Thomas Weller-Poley whose family had long dwelt at Boxted Hall. It was the first election to follow the Franchise Reform Act of 1884 which had increased the electorate by 100 per cent by allowing the franchise to householders and lodgers who had occupied their homes for twelve months prior to registration. Women, of course, were still denied the vote. On polling day there was a riot at Melford and the blame for it can be placed fair and square on the shoulders of the magistrates who were responsible for the distribution of polling stations. Long Melford was allocated two but Glemsford none and in spite of appeals and a petition in the House of Commons nothing was done to alter the situation. The Glemsford voters were obliged to vote at Melford and for many this meant the loss of a day's pay. Small wonder that they saw it as intimidation and an attempt to dissuade them from voting. Many of them had been involved in the coconut mat strike and they saw it as a spiteful retaliation by the magistrates.

The Glemsford voters took it as a challenge and on the morning of polling day some four hundred of them set off on an organised march to Melford. Most of them were voting for the first time in their lives and they truly believed that they were going to change things for the better. When they arrived at the polling station in the Lecture Hall there was much checking and double checking of voters' names which led to delays and suspicion that attempts were being made to deprive them of their vote. Tension mounted and minor incidents snowballed and led to stone throwing which left hardly a window in Hall Street intact. Fighting between opposing parties inevitably broke out and it resulted in a detachment of troops being sent by train from Bury St. Edmunds to quell the disturbance. The Riot Act was read, but complete order was not restored until late in the evening.

Another industry introduced during the nineteenth century was horse-hair weaving and by the 1890s some four hundred persons were employed in this trade which continued into the 1960s.

In 1860 a new school was built at the foot of the Green; until then the Lady Chapel at the church had sufficed since 1670. The church, which had become very run down, was given a thorough but tactful restoration culminating with a new West Tower to commemorate Queen Victoria's Diamond Jubilee.

This all too brief summary of the development of Melford has now brought us to the twentieth century. The village has remained remarkably unscathed in spite of inevitable development and the motor car. With nearby Lavenham it has become an enormous tourist attraction but still manages to retain its identity and copes with the influx of visitors with pride, understanding and care.

The Halls are still standing and their doors are open to anyone willing to pay a moderate admission fee and they are at last being appreciated more fully by an informed and mobile public. The church has become famous throughout the world and quite rightly so, but maintenance of the structure is costly and the Melford folk, aware of their responsibilities, somehow manage to meet the expense.

The misguided closure of the railway in he 1960s is much regretted but parts of the track have been adapted as country walks and the Lavenham stretch has breathtaking views of the Suffolk landscape. Rural public transport is as inadequate in Suffolk as any other county but Melford has good connections by bus with Sudbury, Clare, Lavenham, Bury and Colchester.

It has been said that if you wish to know Suffolk in a day then one should visit Long Melford. I cannot endorse that sentiment strongly enough but once you have been you will want to return and if this volume helps to appreciate the attractions more fully then its purpose has been fulfulled.

THE MAJOR BUILDINGS

INTRODUCTION

There are four major buildings in Melford and three of them are of more than local interest. The first is of course the church because it represents the English Perpendicular style at its best. Those who feel they know the building intimately must have shared my puzzlement when confronted with the strange internal arrangement of the famous Lady Chapel. Then there is the vexed question as to who was responsible for the work on the north side, the only part of the church without inscriptions, and when was it built? I have provided answers to these questions which I firmly believe to be correct and for all I know others may have reached the same conclusions but this is the first time they have appeared in print.

The great mansions of Melford Hall and Kentwell Hall have turned out to be far more important than previously thought. What will surprise many is the fact that Kentwell Hall is for the most part older than her neighbour and must no longer be referred to as an Elizabethan house. Furthermore the one remaining but important fragment of Lutons must now be recognised as a perfect example of a middle fifteenth century brick-built Hall, one of the finest in East Anglia and scarcely altered since the day it was abandoned in favour of the new house.

Melford Hall has turned out to be the younger sister but in historic and architectural terms has been elevated to dizzy heights. The entire Tudor fabric has been much misunderstood in the past and has largely been attributed to William Cordell c. 1550. This attribution must now be discounted for what we have here is a rare and magnificent monastic grange dating from 1520. It was one of the first great houses to be influenced by the Renaissance movement in England and is contemporary with Hampton Court. Apart from that it has now gained Jacobean wings on the west front and a Long Gallery although the latter is now a suite of bedrooms.

The fourth major buildings is the surviving south wing of Melford Place which is so often overlooked because it is not open to the public. It contains a very beautiful early sixteenth century chapel enriched with much carved woodwork of a high standard. Beautifully cared for but threatened with destruction when the remainder of the house was consumed by fire in 1967.

Holy Trinity Church: The west tower was rebuilt by Bodley in 1898–1903. The clerestory and south aisle from the great rebuilding of 1481–84. Flint flushwork at its best but notice the windows of the Martyn chapel, re-used from the earlier church.

The Lady Chapel is an independent eastern extension originally intended as a chantry chapel for the Cloptons. The gables which cut painfully into the east window were not part of the original scheme, they were added when the building became a school in the seventeenth century.

The Martyn chapel: Note the two windows re-used from the earlier chapel. A regrettable act of economy which spoils the rhythm of the south aisle.

The church from the north east showing both Lady Chapels and the brick-built stair turret.

HOLY TRINITY CHURCH

This is one of the most remarkable and beautiful parish churches in England. It has few rivals and once seen is not easily forgotten, whether viewed as a whole from the Bury road or gradually from the narrow passage to the church gate. One cannot fail to be impressed by the extraordinary length of the building, 245 ft. from the west door of the tower to the east wall of the Lady Chapel. The length is emphasised by the eighteen close set and deeply recessed clerestory windows, tall and transomed, but there is also a strong vertical thrust from the tall windows of the aisles which at one time was continued with the help of pinnacles that are now missing. The clerestory on both sides is battlemented, inscribed with the names of donors and dated 1481. The unbattlemented south aisle also carries an inscription and the date, this time 1484.

Most of the windows of the south aisle are grouped in pairs between buttresses but the rhythm is broken at the east end which forms the Martyn chapel. This irritating disturbance is created by two windows with different shaped heads and tracery and they have obviously been re-used from a former chapel probably only a few years old before the church was rebuilt. The rhythm is further disturbed by a third window, similar to the previous run, placed between them. To the east of the Martyn chapel is a low vestry of two bays of c. 1500 and there is another behind and immediately below the great east window.

The Lady Chapel, though joined to the body of the church, is an independent eastern extension originally intended as a chantry chapel for the Cloptons. The walls are low, just over half the height of the aisles, and there are three steep gables when viewed from the rear, the centre being taller. These gables are not an original feature and they date from the time when the chapel was taken over and used as a school in 1670. In the gable ends are three rectangular stone insertions which have probably replaced windows because the roof space was obviously meant to be used. It should be pointed out that the tall gables make nonsense of the very flat roofs inside the chapel.

The windows to the chapel are of the simplest Perpendicular form, just two mullions with trefoiled heads. There is an inscribed parapet but no battlements because they were removed to accommodate the gables. We know they existed because the inscription tells us so:

">... Pray for ye sowle of Richard Loveday, boteleyr with John Clopton, of whose godys this chapell is embaytylled by his excewtors..."

The original chapel probably had a raised centre with pinnacles and battlements and a low battlemented cloister on four sides leaving the great east window unencumbered. The whole of the south side of the church, except the porch, is covered in the most exquisite flint flushwork, i.e. cut and shaped flints set within a dressed stone framework. It is one of the finest displays to be seen on an East Anglian church and it is interesting to see that the later gables of the Lady Chapel are decorated in the same manner.

When moving round to the north side the original tiny Lady Chapel comes into view. It formerly stood apart from the church and was certainly standing before 1439 and although there are no inscriptions it is fully documented through at least six wills and the sums involved reflect the size of the building.

1) 1439: Walter Cobb left ¾d for "... the sustenation and emendation of the chapel of the Blessed Virgin Mary."
2) 1448: John Warawyn left 40/– "... for repair of the Lady Chapel."
3) 1456: Richard Moryell left 2/8d "... for the mending of the Lady Chapel."
4) 1459: Thomas Swyfte left 20d "... to the emendation of the chapel of the Blessed Virgin Mary in the aforesaid churchyard."
5) 1472: Thomas Germayn "... to the repairs of the chapel of Blessed Mary in the churchyard of Melford 12d."

At about this time the reconstruction of the chancel had begun according to a will of John Brokhole dated 1467. This resulted in the chapel becoming annexed.

6) 1473: Robert Barell left 3/4d "... to the emendation of the chapel of the Blessed Mary of the same church annexed."

Above: The original Lady Chapel which became annexed to the main body of the church when the chancel was rebuilt c. 1470. It then became the Clopton Chantry Chapel and was extended slightly to connect with the Clopton Aisle. This is the oldest part of the church and dates from before 1439.

The east window of the Chantry Chapel. The prettiest and the oldest in the church.

The chapel subsequently became the Clopton chantry chapel as we shall see later. It should be noted that the chapel and the whole of the north aisle are devoid of flint flushwork and they are battlemented. Standing well back allows one to see that the aisle is built in two sections and they represent the Clopton or Kentwell chapel and the north aisle of the old church before the rebuilding project masterminded by John Clopton. The eastern four bays form the chapel probably built by William Clopton c. 1440 and the windows are spaced one to a bay and are quite different from those of the aisle although a later window has been inserted above the door. The five bays forming the aisle have paired windows similar to the south side but they are earlier and it seems probable that they were built for William Clopton's son John c. 1465. It is evident that the design of this aisle dictated the style to be adopted for the new work on the south side. The brick stair turret is an obvious addition not envisaged when this north side was built. There are no inscriptions or documents relating to this aisle so the attributions are based on the clues offered by the building and what is known of the Clopton family.

The tower is, alas, not original, its medieval predecessor being struck by lightning in 1709. It was replaced by a brick structure in the classic style but was not considered in keeping with the church. That tower was encased in flint and stone by Bodley in 1898–1903 at a cost of £5,000. Although somewhat 'west country' in style it suits the church well enough but it lacks the East Anglian touch.

Round the tower and we are back on the south side where we began and the entrance is through the porch. This is single storied and tall, the same height as the aisle. It was built in 1481 and has an inscribed parapet but no battlements. There are two tall windows on each side wall and the entrance arch is flanked by a pair of canopied niches with three more above, all of them empty.

Interior

We are not disappointed, it is magnificent and intensely moving. The view from the tower arch is uninterrupted, there being no chancel arch, and it is most impressive. The length of the church can be appreciated fully and the scale and proportions of the whole are as perfect as one would expect for a Perpendicular building such as this. A truly majestic arcade of nine bays with an extended sanctuary, above it the glorious clerestory of eighteen bays each side. The mullions of the windows continue down to the arches below as blank tracery. The roof is worthy of the clerestory, a cambered tie-beam construction of eighteen bays with all the principal rafters arch-braced with open tracery carving in the spandrils. The braces spring from wall posts with small carved figures standing on stone shafts which rise from the apex and sides of the arcade arches.

A close study of the pillars reveals that the first five bays are in fact from the previous church of the fourteenth century. This also applies to the arch moulding. The last four bays to the east are in their details quite different and we know that Clopton rebuilt those on the north and the Martyn family those to the south in c. 1479. From the evidence of the pillars we therefore know that the fourteenth century church had aisles of five bays. Beneath the floor of the south aisle are the footings of its predecessor and they run the length of the five bays only. No footings were discovered on the north side which implies that the present aisle was built on the foundations of the old.

North Aisle

We have already noticed outside that this aisle is in two sections and we can now see that the western section ends where the fourteenth century pillars terminate, at the end of the fifth bay. The four eastern bays with their different windows once flanked the old chancel and this section is called the Clopton or Kentwell Aisle.

The great feature of the north aisle is the fifteenth century glass which miraculously escaped the wanton destruction of the sixteenth and seventeenth centuries. It has been collected from other parts of the church and most of it forms a unique collection of donors' portraits. They all kneel in an attitude of prayer and each figure has been identified and labeled. There are figures of a more religious nature and they should be sought out. Above the door is a beautiful representation of the Virgin Mary with the crucified Christ in her lap. Just beneath is a tiny study of three rabbit heads symbolising the Trinity. There is a representation of St. Edmund with the Abbot of Bury at his feet and others of St. Dominic and St. Peter. Most of this was painted at Norwich but there are two figures of great beauty, St. Gabriel and St. Michael, which are believed to have originated from London. There is a collection of later glass as well.

The porch c. 1481. The three niches above the door were probably meant for statues of the Trinity. Apart from the plinth it is devoid of flushwork.

Below: North aisle: Nottingham alabaster panel from a reredos depicting the Adoration of the Magi c. 1350 and therefore a relic from the earlier church and in pristine condition because it was hidden beneath the chancel floor for centuries.

The Clopton chantry chapel: beautiful niches above Clopton's tomb, obviously meant to contain statues of the twelve apostles. Above them is part of the scroll cornice with verses from Lidgate's poem.

The Clopton chantry chapel: Clopton's tomb between the sanctuary and the chapel, the most prestigious position in the church which suddenly became available when the earlier Lady Chapel was annexed to the chancel.

Sir William Cordell's Tomb c. 1582. Excellent work and probably by Cornelius Cure.

The Lady Chapel: Note the west wall of the 'shrine' area, the canopied niche at the corner, and the beautifully moulded arches of the arcade.

Before passing through the screen into the Clopton aisle one should study the Nottingham alabaster panel set into the wall. It was found beneath the floor and is remarkably unscathed. It dates from c. 1350 and depicts a most beautiful representation of the Adoration of the Magi. It probably formed part of a reredos but whether it was lost during the rebuilding of the chancel or was deliberately concealed at a later date is a matter for debate. In the parish records for the year 1548, when the church was being stripped of its furnishings, is the following:

"Sold to Master Clopton. The greates images about the church and chapel of alabaster for 3.0d.
Sold to Mr. Clopton, the altar of alabaster in our Ladies Chapel.
And left unto Master Clopton ij stonys at the end of the altar in Master Clopton's aisle and the table of alabaster in the said aisle and a little table in St. Annes Chapel."

In the Clopton aisle or chapel is further evidence that the aisle predates the re-building of c. 1481. Set against the wall on the north side is the tomb of William Clopton, the father of John who died in 1446. He is shown as a knight in armour lying on a tomb chest and above him is a shallow arch crowned with a row of cresting. Built into the corner of the tomb is a pillar stoup for the use of those entering through the door which proves that it has always been in this position. Both tomb chest and effigy are carved in clunch, a very soft material easily damaged. Needless to say the tomb has been restored and looks a little too spruce. On the floor are some tomb slabs with brasses and two of them date from 1420. Another two depicting women in butterfly head-dress of c. 1480 and a third of Francis Clopton who died in 1558.

Against the east wall of this chapel was an altar and there is a double squint which enabled the priest to have a clear view of the high altar when officiating at Mass. It was inserted after the new chancel was built. To the left is the small doorway which will take us into the Clopton chantry chapel.

The Clopton Chantry Chapel

The door from the aisle leads into a tiny lobby with a fireplace on the left and a flat ceiling in the form of a fan vault just inches above one's head. The chapel was much smaller when it was the Lady Chapel, the lobby and the area beneath the cantilevered west wall are extensions created when it became a chantry. Facing the altar the wall on our right is treated sumptuously in carved stone. Beneath the cantilevered section is a seat within a deeply recessed arch and immediately alongside is the tomb of John Clopton and his wife. A plain tomb chest of Purbeck Marble with a frieze of three shields decorating the front. Above it is a depressed ogee arch which is open to the chancel next door. On the soffit of the arch is a painting of the Risen Christ with a Latin text issuing from his mouth which, translated, reads: "Everyone who lives and believes in me shall never die." Also on the soffit a much faded painting of John Clopton and his wife. At the apex of the arch is an image stool.

East of the tomb, but 'en suite' as it were, is a two-bay sedilia and then a pillar piscina with a credence shelf above it. This is all linked together, first by a frieze of painted shields showing various arms of the Cloptons, then above that a series of twelve beautifully carved canopied niches, obviously intended for the twelve apostles.

The roof is flat pitched and the ridge beam and rafters are decorated with scrolls bearing the words 'IHU Mercy' and 'Gramercy'. There is a deep cornice in the form of a folded scroll, each fold linked with a rope and vine motif. On the scroll in black letters is a long poem ascribed to John Lidgate the poet monk from Bury Abbey who died in c. 1450. There are many traces of other paintings on the walls.

The east window above the altar is the prettiest in the church, seven lights, transomed, with a row of six multifoiled circles beneath the almost flat arch. This is the oldest surviving window in the church and in the centre lower light is one of the rarest pieces of stained glass. It dates from 1450 and shows Christ cruficied on the petals of a lily.

The Sanctuary

The impressive and large reredos was given to the church by the mother of the Rector Charles Martin in 1877, (according to the church guide.) It is made of Caen stone and depicts the Crucifixion after Durer. It replaced an eighteenth century pedimented reredos displaying the Ten Commandments from which only the Hanoverian carved arms have survived and are exhibited at the other end of the church.

To the north of the altar is Clopton's tomb which in medieval days served as an Easter sepulchre. A special framework was erected around it and the reserved sacrament was housed here throughout the Easter festival. It was considered a great honour and a benediction to have one's tomb so used. Opposite is the stately tomb of Sir William Cordell, of Melford Hall. He died in 1581 and is buried here with his wife, but there is only the one effigy, that of Sir William, shown as a knight-at-arms, lying on a partly rolled mat. Above him are two coffered arches supported by columns with rich capitals.

Two niches at the back and one at each side of the tomb contain figures representing Prudence, Justice, Temperance and Fortitude, all of whom served him well in his lifetime. The tomb is constructed from a mixture of alabaster and marble and it stands on a Purbeck marble base. Obviously the work of a master mason and both style and date suggest Cornelius Cure.

Before leaving the chancel one should note the four image stools just to the east of the Clopton tomb, they are part of the original decoration.

Martyn Chapel

This lies to the south of the chancel and contains the Purbeck marble tomb chest of Lawrence Martyn who died in 1460, and his two wives. On the floor are the tomb slabs of other Martyns. One has the brasses of Roger Martyn, d. 1615, and his two wives Ursula and Margaret. Beneath each wife is a brass showing the children she bore him. Another slab has brasses to Richard Martyn, d. 1624, and his three wives. Other slabs have had their brasses removed.

When this chapel was rebuilt by the Martyn family it housed an altar flanked by two gilt tabernacles which reached from floor to ceiling. In one was the image of Our Lady of Pity and in the other a representation of Christ with a bowl in his hands signifying the world. They were destroyed or removed in the reign of Edward VI. The screen at the west end of the chapel marks the position of the medieval Rood Screen which stretched right across the church. Not a splinter has survived.

Both south and north aisles have good roofs, tie beams with alternate principals arch braced with pierced tracery carving. The bracing springs from carved wood figures on stone brackets. At the west end is the fifteenth century font, again of Purbeck marble, with its eight sides decorated with shields.

The Lady Chapel

To reach it we are obliged to leave the church, in itself a remarkable thing. From the gabled exterior we are led to expect a small aisled chapel, like a miniature church, but what we find is quite different. It is in fact a small central chapel surrounded on four sides by an ambulatory or cloister, a unique arrangement for a Lady Chapel but not so surprising when we remember that it was intended as a chantry chapel with a tomb in the centre. What caused Clopton to abandon it in favour of the old Lady Chapel was the death of his wife before this building was completed and consecrated. It is quite clear from his will that she was dead before 1494. The old Lady Chapel, having become annexed to the chancel, presented him with the opportunity of being buried in the most prestigious position in the church, the north sanctuary. So the exchange was made, Clopton took the Lady Chapel for his chantry and the parish gained a new one, strange in plan for its purpose and still unfinished when Clopton died.

The central chapel, or shrine area, is open to the cloister on the north and south with a low arcade of three beautifully moulded arches. Above them, on the inside, is a frieze of blank tracery with a double tier on the west wall. Behind the altar is a solid wall with a sunken arch which was probably meant to frame a reredos. The opposite or west wall is pierced by a doorway flanked by two small windows of two lights. The moulding of the doorway is decorated with fleurons and there is a frieze of shields above it on the cloister side, similar to those in the chantry. Inside the shrine area are six canopied niches, unfortunately empty. The roof here is higher than the cloister and it is of the cambered tie-beam variety.

The cloister has an excellent cambered roof with the principal rafters arch braced and a scroll and rope cornice which is another echo from the chantry. The bracing springs from small carved figures; on the chapel side they stand on stone shafts but on the outer walls they rest on stone corbels. At each corner of the shrine, facing the cloister, is another canopied niche and just above them is the diagonal arch bracing which emphasises the ambulatory effect. The windows reach half way down the wall but the moulding continues to the floor to frame shallow stone seats. Beneath one is a multiplication table which reminds us that this building was used as a school for nearly two hundred years and after that as a coal store!

The Lady Chapel: The arch braced tie-beam roof. Note the angled tie-beam which emphasises the ambulatory effect of the cloister.

The Lady Chapel: Niches and blank tracery within the 'shrine' area originally intended to house John Clopton's tomb.

The inscription on the parapet makes it quite clear that apart from the battlements, which no longer exist, the entire cost of this chapel was paid for by John Clopton. Had his intentions been carried out to the full, one wonders what his tomb would have been like and whether he intended the cloister to house those of his descendants.

The stone carving in both the Lady Chapel and the chantry is very similar to work at Burwell church in Cambridgeshire. It is known that the Master Mason employed there was the King's Mason, Reginald Ely. The similarities between the two churches are many, especially the clerestories and roofs, and although we have no documents to prove the theory, comparative study strongly suggests that he was in charge of the work at Long Melford.

Inscriptions

The inscriptions above the walls are given here for those interested:

Clerestory north:
> Pray for ye sowlis of Robert Spar'we and Marion his wife and for Thom' Cowper, and Ma'el his wife, of quos goodis Mastr Gilis Dent, John Clopton, John Smyth, and Roger Smyth, With ye help of ye weel disposyd me' of this town dede these se'en archis new repare 1481.

Clerestory south:
> Pray for the sowlis of Rogere Moryell, Margarate and Kateryn his wyffis, of whose goodis the seyd Kateryn, John Clopton, Master Wyllem Qwaytis and John Smyth ded these VI archis new repare: and did make the tabill at the hye awtere, anno domini millesimo quadrigentesimo octogesio p'mo. Pray for ye sowel of Thomas Couper ye wych ye II arche ded repare. Pray for ye sowl of Law. Martin and Marion his wif.

Porch:
> Pray for ye sowlis of William Clopton, Margy and Margy his wifis and for ye sowle of Alice Clopton and for John Clopton and for alle thoo sowles yt ye seyd John is bo'nde to prey for.

South aisle:
> Pray for ye sowl of Rog Moriell of who goods yis arch was made. Pray for the sowl of John Keche, and for his fad'

and Mod' of whose goodis yis arche was made. Pray for ye sowle of Thos Elys and Jone his wife, and for ye good sped of Jone Elys maks h'of. Pray for ye sowl of John Pie and Aly his wife, of whose goodis yis arch was made and yes twey wy'sdowy glasid. Pray for ye soulis of John Distr and Alis, and for ye good sped of John Distr and X'pian maks hof.

South chapel:

Pray for ye soulis of Laurens Martyn and Marion his wyffe, Elizabeth Martyn a'd Jone, and for ye good estat of Richard Martyn and Roger Martyn and ye wyvis and alle ye childri of whose goodis made 1484.

Lady Chapel:

Pray for ye sowle of John Hyll, and for ye sowle of John Clopton Esqwyer and pray for ye sowle of Richard Loveday, boteleyr with John Clopton, of whose godys this chapell ys imbaytylled by his excewtors. Pray for the soulis of William Clopton Esqwyer, Margery and Marg'y his wyfis and for all ther parentis and childri, and for ye sowle of Alice Clopton, and for John Clopton and for all his childri and for all ye soulis that the said John is bonde to p'y for, which did yis chapel new repare anno domo MCCCCLXXXXVI (1496).

Christ sit testis hec me no'exhibuisse ut merear laudes, sed ut spiritus memoretur.

Dimensions

The dimensions of the church are as follows:

Length of nave:	152 ft. 6 ins. From the tower arch to the east wall behind the altar.
Height of nave:	41 ft. 6 ins.
Length of aisles:	135 ft. 4 ins.
Height of aisles:	24 ft.
Total length of church and Lady Chapel:	245 ft.

KENTWELL HALL

My first visit to this house was in the late 1950s when it was the home of Mr. Charles Starkie Bence and at that time it had an atmosphere of genteel decline, sad but romantic. My second visit was to attend the sale of the house and its contents following the death of the owner in 1969, a melancholy experience heightened by the knowledge that the house was unlikely ever to become a home again. Most of those present were well aware that only a few miles away the stately Rushbrooke Hall, very similar to Kentwell, was standing derelict and unwanted.

In 1971 it was announced that a lawyer named Patrick Phillips had bought the house and gardens with the expressed intention of restoring them to their former Elizabethan glory. The general opinion was that he was either very rich or completely eccentric or both. He turned out to be neither and within a short space of time demonstrated that he was courageous, imaginative, romantic and a genius. His courage to take on such a task is unquestioned, especially as it is being done without the aid of government grants, he being determined that Kentwell Hall must pay its own way. Imaginative he certainly is, as witnessed by the fact that from the start the public have had complete access to observe the restoration as it progressed. Romantic without doubt, because he fell in love with the house and fortunately so did his wife. Together they have achieved a remarkable success because thousands of people return again and again to see how the work is coming along. That is where the genius shows because it is the house we come to see and not the contents. Furnishing a place of this size is no easy task, especially as priority has been given to the restoration of the fabric and gardens. Regular visitors will have noticed that the furnishings have improved a good deal of late and I hope that the owners will accept that as a compliment and not an impertinence. Visiting Kentwell is an odd and satisfying experience, that we are welcome is beyond question but the visitor never leaves without feeling somehow involved in the enterprise.

The entrance fee is remarkably reasonable considering the fact that practically all the rooms are on view and there is unhindered access to the beautiful gardens. In place of a guide-book one can purchase a folio of information sheets, a very sensible idea which allows the information to be constantly updated as the work progresses. The folio contains a compre-

Kentwell Hall: The Moat House, the original Great Hall of the old mansion of Lutons. A remarkable brick building of c. 1435.

hensive list of previous owners, a detailed description of the restoration work so far and an instruction sheet to guide you round the house and gardens. Apart from this every room has an information sheet within it. There is no hastle, one is encouraged to linger and browse. There are also refreshment and toilet facilities.

The recorded history of Kentwell is long and reaches back to Saxon times. Over the years it has swallowed up at least five smaller manors, the most important of which was Lutons. There has been much confusion as to which manor was situated where but lately it has become obvious that the present Kentwell Hall stands within the moated site of Lutons. The original Kentwell Manor was situated about one mile further north-west. As this book is mainly concerned with what exists today we will pick up the story in 1373 when the manor was purchased from the Gower family on behalf of Katherine Mylde who was a minor. Nine years later she was married to Sir Thomas Clopton and within one year had presented him with a son and heir who was to become fatherless within a few months. She very soon married again, this time to Sir William Tendring of Stoke-by-Nayland and the Howards, Dukes of Norfolk, were descended from this union. The young William Clopton was raised with the Tendrings at Stoke-by-Nayland and he was just twenty when his mother died leaving him owner of the Melford estate. It is more than likely that the manor house at Lutons was under reconstruction in anticipation of the event. In 1415, at the age of thirty two, he fought at the battle of Agincourt and there can be no doubt that before he died in 1446 he was responsible for the building of the Kentwell aisle in the church where he was buried. His son John who succeeded him was the man who masterminded the rebuilding project some years later and by doing so merely completed the task his father had begun.

I am convinced that William Clopton was also the builder of the Great Hall at Lutons during the last ten years of his life. It still stands today alongside the west wing of the later house and is now known as The Moat House. It is solidly constructed of red brick and is open to the pitch of the gable where the blackened timbers tell us that it had a central hearth with no chimney. In the centre of the west wall is a tall alcove forming a garderobe with arrow slit windows and on either side are windows placed very high up which was usual for a hall of this type. At the north end are two brick doorways which lead into

Kentwell Hall: Interior of the Great Hall of Lutons showing the two doorways leading to the Buttery and Kitchen in the timber-framed section.

the timber framed buttery and kitchen and the slots in the main ridge beam show clearly where the dividing wall stood. This timber framed unit was partly rebuilt in brick when a further bakehouse was added a few years later. Above the service rooms are two chambers which housed the retainers but the parlour and great chamber no longer exist. 1436 may seem an early date for such a brick building but that same material was used at Little Wenham Hall as early as 1270 and is recognised as the earliest example of a brick built house in England. This Hall at Lutons would have been the nucleus of a range of buildings which probably formed a courtyard house with a gatehouse on the site of the present staircase hall of the later house. The recent discovery of some earlier footings at the east end of the main block certainly proves that a range existed along the north side. This would also add substance to the long-held theory that before the avenue was planted in the seventeenth century the main approach to the house was from the Bury road closer to Bridge Street. When John Clopton inherited the estate in 1446 the manor house was already a substantial residence. Other brick built homes contemporary with Lutons were Caister Castle in Norfolk, the home of the Fastolf family, and Tattershall Castle in Lincolnshire. Across the road at Melford Hall there are definite remains of an earlier brick house which must have co-existed with Lutons.

We now have to decide just who was responsible for the new building we see today and this is not quite as simple as at first appears. What looks to be a pure Elizabethan house with a main hall block and far projecting wings is in fact of different dates and the deceptive symmetry was arrived at almost by accident. The main block was the first section to be constructed but to arrive at its original form we must take away the top floor entirely, including that of the porch, remove the tall bay window on the left and take away the wings leaving a short stump on the right which served as a staircase tower. This leaves us with a classic hall house constructed entirely from brick but on a much grander scale than the older Lutons. In its original form the porch gave access to the Screens' Passage with a minstrel gallery above. To the left of the screen was a service room with a staircase giving access to the gallery and at least two rooms for guests. To the right of the screen lay the Great Hall but this time the roof was flat pitched with richly carved timbers and the central hearth had given way to a large fireplace set in the centre of the back wall. The windows were placed high up as usual to allow for the rich wall hangings below and at the far end, opposite the screen and gallery, was a dais lit by an enormous mullioned and transomed bay window. Close by was a doorway leading to the parlour and the staircase giving access to the Great Chamber. All the windows were glazed and there were fireplaces in all rooms. In short we are looking at a house built in the last quarter of the fifteenth century and the builder can only be John Clopton.

Because of what we know of him and the position he held in society it is inconceivable that he would have lived content with the primitive style of living in the old house. He was a man of great wealth who moved in the highest circles and from his work at the church we know he was a man of taste and refinement. The superb and rich collection of stained glass portraits and the lavish display of heraldry which he commissioned for the windows is ample evidence that he was also a proud man and very well connected. When he died in 1497 the house was very much as described above but much of the old house was also standing and still in use.

When Sir William Clopton II inherited the house he was forty seven and held a prominent position in East Anglian society. He was to marry three times and held the manor for thirty three years. His third marriage brought more wealth into the family and it is possible, but by no means certain, that he began work on the west wing. During his tenure the Abbot of Bury was rebuilding Melford Hall with its Renaissance turrets.

Sir William's son John also married a rich heiress, Catherine Roydon, but as he was close on sixty when he inherited Lutons it is unlikely that he would have bothered to extend the house. His father's will especially mentions 'all the hangings within the Hall, Parlour, and Great Chamber". He also left Lutons to his wife for her lifetime so it may have been some time before John gained full access. After just a few years he died in 1541 leaving the estate to his son William III and once again the will especially refers to: "The hangings, bed and tester in my Lordys chamber, also the hangings of my hall and parlour" which seems to confirm that the house was little changed from John Clopton's time.

William III was undoubtedly the man who built the two wings and it is obvious that work commenced very soon after his father's death. He was just thirty, married, and with a large family. We know very little about this man except that he was wealthy and religious and seemed to have spent most of his time improving the estate and the house. He was obviously a family man who was cautious and preferred to keep away from politics and controversy during that most troublesome and dangerous period. Just before his death his father had purchased those parts of Monk's Manor which had been leased by the family for years following the dissolution of the monasteries. He was distantly related to Anne Boleyn and the Dukes of Norfolk, so he must have taken more than a little interest in the strange goings on at court. He also seems to have remained a Catholic and must have been very disturbed as the church was gradually stripped of the ornaments which his family had so generously donated. In the parish records for 1548 we read that he purchased back certain alabaster altars and images though what became of them is a mystery.

We can see from his work at Kentwell Hall that he was completely unaffected by the Renaissance movement in architecture. His new wings are in the English perpendicular domestic style with mullioned and transomed windows with arched lights. The only difference between them and the main block is that the courtyard facades and the gable ends are completely symmetric; in that at least he was very much up to date. There is not a single classical motif of any kind, not even on the turrets which, like Melford Hall have square.bases that become octagonal. Their windows are arched and the ogee domes have no decoration. The one feature that hints at a break away from tradition is the absence of battlements from the parapets. Because of his conservatism when building the wings we may safely assume that he was not responsible for the upper floor of the main block which was added to provide a long gallery. The spacing of the mullions in the windows is different from the others and the lights are not arched. The gallery was probably added by his son Francis after 1562 and is therefore the first Elizabethan structure to appear at Kentwell. Its construction entailed the building of a new staircase to the left of the Screens' Passage where the service room had been. To light the staircase a large bay window was built to match that of the hall which then made the facade very nearly symmetrical. Kentwell Hall was at last completed and the exterior has changed very little since. It is, of course, a Tudor house and not Elizabethan as it has so often been described. One should not try to compare the hall and wings plan with that at Melford Hall because when this house was finally completed the latter was still quadrangular.

The interior has been remodelled several times and this has been the cause of much heart-searching in recent years. Just what does one keep when restoring such a house as this? What should be preserved or restored and what should be removed? Thankfully the owners have got it just about right.

Interior

Tudor Period

Much of the Tudor work has been restored, especially in the west wing which was built to house the kitchens, pantry, Butler's room, Housekeeper's room etc. with a series of lodgings with garderobes on the first floor and a retainers' gallery beneath the roof. A wealth of timber-framing has been exposed on the ground floor and the general plan is of a corridor with rooms opening off. One room is complete with original oak wainscot and several original fireplaces and windows have been uncovered and carefully restored.

In the main block, apart from the fenestration and the shell, there is very little Tudor work exposed. The same applies to the east wing although at the time of writing the top floor is closed off for 'work in progress'.

The most interesting early work, fully exposed and very exciting is the Moat House or Great Hall of Old Lutons. This could easily be overlooked and should on no account be missed.

Seventeenth Century 1676–1683

In 1676 the house was purchased from Sir Thomas Darcy by a lawyer, Sir Thomas Robinson. To this man we owe the splendid lime avenue which is such a lovely feature of Kentwell. He was also responsible for substantial alterations to the interior. From this period belongs the superb open well staircase in the east wing. This is an impressive structure with robust turned balusters and finely shaped banister rail. I suspect that structurally the staircase hall is original c.1475 but Hopper worked on it in the nineteenth century.

Richard Moore 1782–1823

In various parts of the house there are Georgian features such as dentil cornices, fireplaces, doorways, etc., and most of them were introduced during the ownership of Richard Moore.

The Moat Bedroom in the west wing is very much a room from this period and the mantlepiece is decorated with the Moore arms. I feel certain that the Billiard Room and the Library in the east wing were created at the same time but Hopper has been given the credit.

Hopper's Alterations 1826

In 1823 the house was purchased by Robert Hart Logan, a Scotsman who emigrated to Canada as a young man and made his fortune from timber. Tradition has it that a fire gutted the central block in 1826 but not much evidence has been found to support the story. It was certainly gutted but by Thomas Hopper the architect who had been earlier engaged by Sir William Parker at Melford Hall. With Sir William Parker the architect was working for a man with impeccable taste who knew exactly what he wanted which resulted in work of a very high standard. At Kentwell we are faced with a curious mixture of Scottish Baronial and English Jacobean which in its original state was very sombre and somewhat overpowering and completely at odds with the spirit of the house. It smacks of the newly rich and I suspect that once again Hopper carried out his client's wishes to the last letter.

The structural alterations to the Great Hall involved the removal of the original screen and gallery and replacing it with the present nineteenth century version. An eighteenth century fireplace had replaced the Tudor version and was allowed to remain but the ceiling was completely reconstructed. Hopper's decor is an odd mixture of styles with Jacobean motifs above the dado and Gothic below. The ceiling with its hammer beams, pendants and wall posts is entirely of plaster and is a close copy of Audley End in Essex — Jacobean again. All of this is coloured to simulate oak. The dado was also painted in the same manner but is now an ivory colour which is most successful and much easier to live with. There is a splash of colour from the recently uncovered red brick wall above the gallery where two original doorways have been revealed. There is a fine collection of stained glass from several periods in the windows assembled by Hart Logan. The heavily ornamented doors are very Scottish Baronial but the doorways are English Perpendicular. There must have been a great temptation to remove every vestige of Hopper's work but the compromise is successful and it is a very pleasant room.

Above: Kentwell Hall: South front showing the main block with far projecting wings and central porch. Not Elizabethan as at first appears but c. 1470–1545.

Kentwell Hall: Porch and great bay of the hall by John Clopton c. 1470. The top floor of porch and hall forming a long gallery added by his great grandson William Clopton c. 1562.

Kentwell Hall: East wing from the Cedar Lawn. The large window to the right of the chimney marks the position of the staircase hall, which formed part of the original build of c. 1470.

Kentwell Hall: East Turret, square base becoming octagonal at parapet level. Unlike those at Melford Hall this has Gothic windows c. 1545.

Kentwell Hall: North front. Chimney to the left marks the Parlour with Great Chamber above of John Clopton. Middle chimney served his Great Hall. Top floor formed the Long Gallery of William Clopton.

Kentwell Hall: Hopper's Screen and dado of c. 1823 in the Great Hall. Eighteenth century fireplace and recently uncovered doorways in the gallery.

Passing through the Screens' Passage we come to the main dining room which again is two-storied and fills the space occupied first by a service room and later by a staircase. It is a room created by Hopper and much of his work has survived. We must be grateful to the owners for that because in its original colours it must have been very difficult to live with. Once again we have a mixture of styles and they are separated by a frieze at doorway height. The upper walls are decorated with a series of large blank Tudor arches with a narrow cornice of foliage above. Below the frieze runs a blank arcade of Jacobean arches and pilasters. The frieze is painted to simulate oak and is decorated with a trailing vine. The upper walls have retained Hopper's decoration of strapwork on a red background but elsewhere his colours have mercifully been changed to lighter tones. The ceiling is once again Jacobean with panels and pendants. The outstanding feature is the massive fireplace and overmantle in the Gothic style and carved from grey marble from Bardoglio in Italy. It is copied from one in the Bishop's Palace at Exeter which is dated 1485, coincidentally close to the date of Kentwell.

Above these two rooms was the Long Gallery, a necessary feature of Elizabethan and Jacobean houses of this size. It has suffered the same fate as that at Melford Hall and now forms a range of bedrooms but the gallery effect is sustained in the corridor with its bays which overlooks the court.

The Library and Billiard Room occupy the Ground Floor of the east wing and they have been attributed to Hopper and not without reason. I find it difficult to agree with the attribution. These two rooms are the most satisfying in the house and they are quietly Georgian in a decidedly masculine way. There are no fancy frills, no sophisticated Greek details as at Melford Hall and if a comparison has to be made then I would liken them to the rooms of a private club in St. James. The Library has a screen formed by a pair of scagliola columns and a good marble fireplace. Doorcases and other features in both rooms are in the late Georgian style and seem more likely to have been introduced by Richard Moore between 1790 and 1800. The undisciplined display of mixed architectural motifs in the Great Hall and Main Dining Room are too much at variance with the controlled elegance of the east wing. They must surely be the tastes of two different men. The attribution to Hopper is supported by the fact that he was definitely responsible for the rooms being heightened by some two feet

Kentwell Hall: Garden delights, the gazebo and bridge by the Moat House.

*Kentwell Hall: The seventeenth century Dovehouse.
Reputed to be one of the largest in East Anglia.*

in 1826. The carpenters who laid the new floors above left dated notes which confirm the fact. On the other hand it is asking too much to consider a house of this size not having a Library in the eighteenth century. With a house as old as Kentwell a dispute about a thirty year period in its long history may seem paltry but that is the effect it has on you. The more one knows the more one wants to know and that is why people keep returning to the house to see the progress.

The staircase hall acts as an ante-room to the Billiard Room and it would seem that Hopper was responsible for the plasterwork decoration here. The centre ceiling rose and the cornice have been repainted successfully in 1977. The ground floor area has plaster panelling painted to match the oak of the staircase. It also appears that Hopper has altered the staircase itself, probably to execute a realignment. John Clopton's Parlour is now a handsome early nineteenth century Drawing Room while his Great Chamber and another room above now form the State Bedroom. This has a deep coved ceiling with delicate plaster moulding more in a late seventeenth century style but again attributed to Hopper.

The Gardens

There is something peculiarly but pleasantly haunting about the gardens which defies description. The information sheet in the folio guide should be consulted before setting off to explore the numerous delights which include: a yew walk, a yew lawn, a splendid walled garden with forty varieties of apple, a sunken garden, a fishpond and moat, and the splendid seventeenth century dove house. The visitor has unhindered access to all of it and the house can be studied from all angles which allows the discerning eye to detect the minor alterations down the centuries.

MELFORD HALL

This very important house is now a National Trust property although still the home of Sir Richard Hyde Parker, 12th Baronet, whose family have lived here since 1786. It has a complex building history which has never been satisfactorily explained. Outward appearances tend to classify it as the standard Elizabethan 'E' type manor-house but there are external features which clearly belong to an earlier period. Apart from that we have to consider the original plan which was quadrangular, in the style of a late medieval college with gatehouses to the east and west. The Elizabethan appearance was arrived at through modifications over two hundred years. Until now it has been accepted that the man responsible for the bulk of the house was Sir William Cordell who began leasing the manor from the Crown in 1547 and was to acquire it outright from Queen Mary in 1554 in the second year of her brief reign. Before Cordell it had been the property of the Abbey of St. Edmundsbury, a Benedictine abbey and one of the wealthiest in the kingdom.

Because of subsequent alterations certain features which usually enable one to date a building fairly accurately have been removed. The whole of the fenestration was altered in the eighteenth century and some of it restored about a century later. The Great Hall was subject to an internal reconstruction in 1813–15 which removed valuable clues leaving precious little to guide us there either. Recent renovations however have uncovered supporting evidence that the attribution to Cordell for the bulk of the work is no longer acceptable.

The turrets are an outstanding feature of the house and they have been assigned to the middle of the sixteenth century but one must question this. There are two at the ends of the long wings and four along the west front. They rise from square bases but become octagonal at parapet level. There are small windows on each face just beneath the ogee shaped domes, they are square and not arched and form a lantern. Then there are small lunettes to the domes which carry a fan shaped motif, an Italian Renaissance feature which appears abundantly at Layer Marney Tower in Essex, a building constructed in 1520 and barely twenty five miles away. However it is the grouping of the turrets along the west front which is of great interest and has been insufficiently studied.

The west front has a complicated rhythm completely at variance with the east front and apart from some minor alterations in 1813 has always been accepted as Cordell's work of c. 1550 but this must now be discounted. There is a drawing of the house on a survey map by Samuel Pierse dated 1613 which shows the quadrangular mansion but the three storied wings which flank the west front are conspicuous by their absence. The four turrets and the chimneys in between are however very much in evidence and this throws an entirely new light on the structural history of the house and would seem to confirm a date of c. 1520.

The west front minus the three storied wings presents to us a typical early Tudor gatehouse facade remarkably similar in plan to Wolsey's at Hampton Court which was constructed c. 1515—20. A close look at the brickwork between the centre turrets will show that the doorway and first floor window were originally much broader. Until 1813 the walls flanking this centre were set back a few feet adding emphasis to the entrance. The outer turrets are structurally thinner which tells us that the facade extended a few feet to the north and south.

The gatehouse was an important feature of fortified manor houses and castles in earlier years but as the need for fortifications diminished they developed into the focal point of a show front and often served as a backdrop for a display of heraldry. This gatehouse is contemporary with Layer Marney, Hampton Court and Hengrave Hall near Bury. St. Edmunds. It differs from them in one important aspect for at Melford it has become a grand porch or ceremonial entrance leading directly into the Screens' Passage of the Great Hall. There was another gatehouse forming the east front demolished in the eighteenth century but like Hampton Court and Layer Marney it gave access to the centre court.

The grouping of the turrets on the west front is typically English but the complete lack of Gothic ornament and the Renaissance detail of the domes lifts this facade above the norm and places Melford Hall firmly in the ranks of very important buildings. In plan and detail it is correct for 1520 but wrong for 1550 and there can be no doubt that this is the work of Abbot Reeve and bearing in mind that there are two further turrets at the ends of the long wings it becomes increasingly apparent that the whole of the Tudor structure is his apart from the east porch. Abbot Reeve was the last Abbot of Bury and was elected

Melford Hall: West Front with the four turrets which formed the Gatehouse facade of Abbot Reeve's Hall. The walls between the outer and inner turrets were moved forward in 1813–15. Flanking the turrets are the three storied Jacobean wings.

Melford Hall: The East Front showing the turrets which flanked the East Gatehouse, demolished in 1730–40.

to that post in 1515. For centuries Melford Hall was used as a retreat for the personal use of the Abbots and as Reeve was a native of Melford he probably set about rebuilding the hall soon after his election. He was Lord of the Manor of Melford but at that time the most respected man in the village was William Clopton whose family had been mainly responsible for the rebuilding of the church and who lived in a very substantial house. Melford Hall had to be rebuilt on a grand scale to impress the villagers and to remind them that young John Reeve was now a very powerful man and their Lord. He no doubt enjoyed its facilities for some time before leasing it to Dame Frances Pennington for thirty years in 1534. She remained in possession after the suppression of the Abbey but was obliged to pay her rent into the Royal Exchequer until she vacated the premises in 1547.

In the cellar beneath the main range are structural remains of an earlier house also constructed with brick, probably between 1450–80, though an earlier date cannot be ruled out. It appears to have consisted of a main hall block with a northern cross-wing. There are indications which suggest that the cross-wing had a form of undercroft so the upper floor may have formed a chapel. On either side of the present north wing is a visible join which points to the cross-wing having been incorporated in the new work.

The east porch is the only structure that can be reliably attributed to Cordell and it is an interesting classical composition in the Renaissance style but this time it is the French version. There is a round headed doorway with a pedimented window above and they are flanked by both Ionic and Doric pilasters. The porch is crowned with a version of the fan motif and also carries his initials. The pedimented window arrived in England from France and first appeared at Somerset House in London c. 1547–51. We must assume that when this porch was constructed the entrance on the west front became secondary enabling the boundary wall on that side to be built. There are some lead rain water heads bearing Cordell's crest of a cockatrice but they could have been placed there at any time between 1547 and 1581. The house is constructed throughout with local red bricks laid in the English bond and later alterations were carried out with the same bricks and bonding which has led to some confusion.

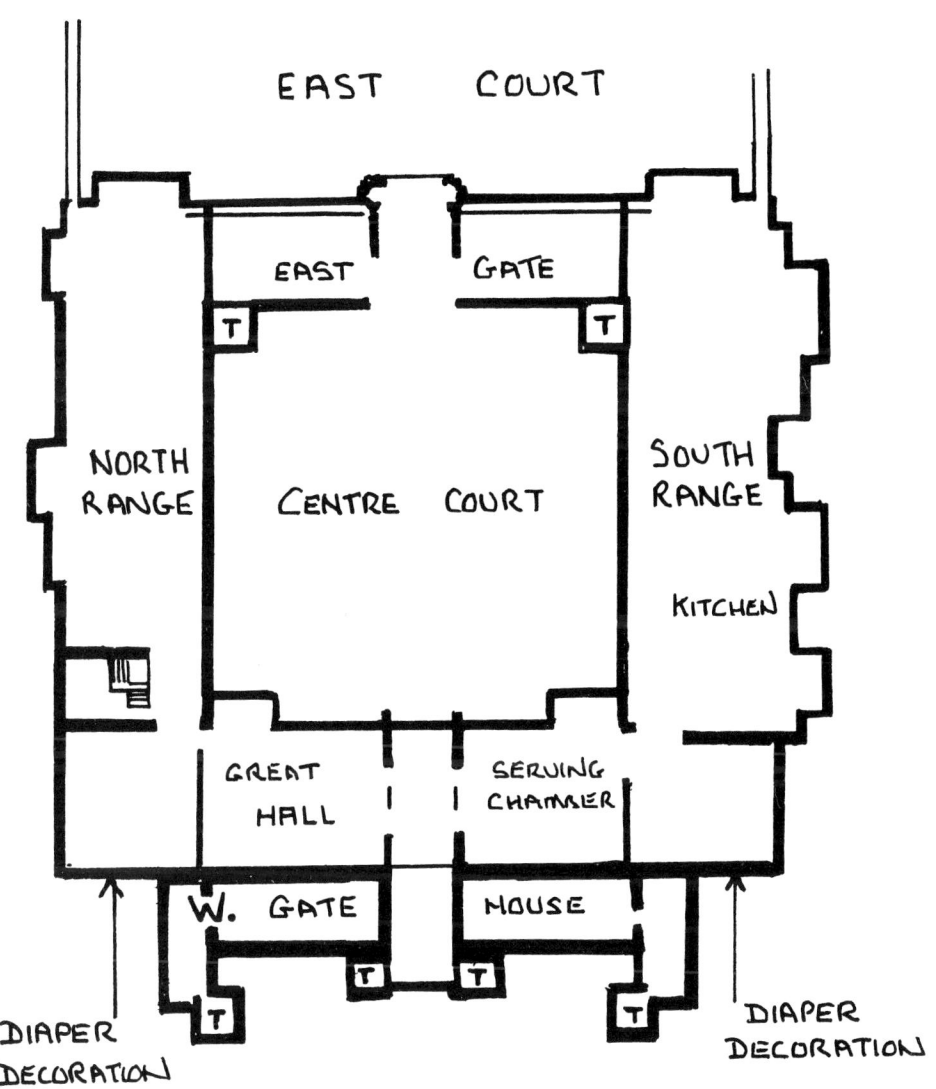

Melford Hall: Outline plan showing Abbot Reeve's Hall with Western gatehouse before the Jacobean extensions.

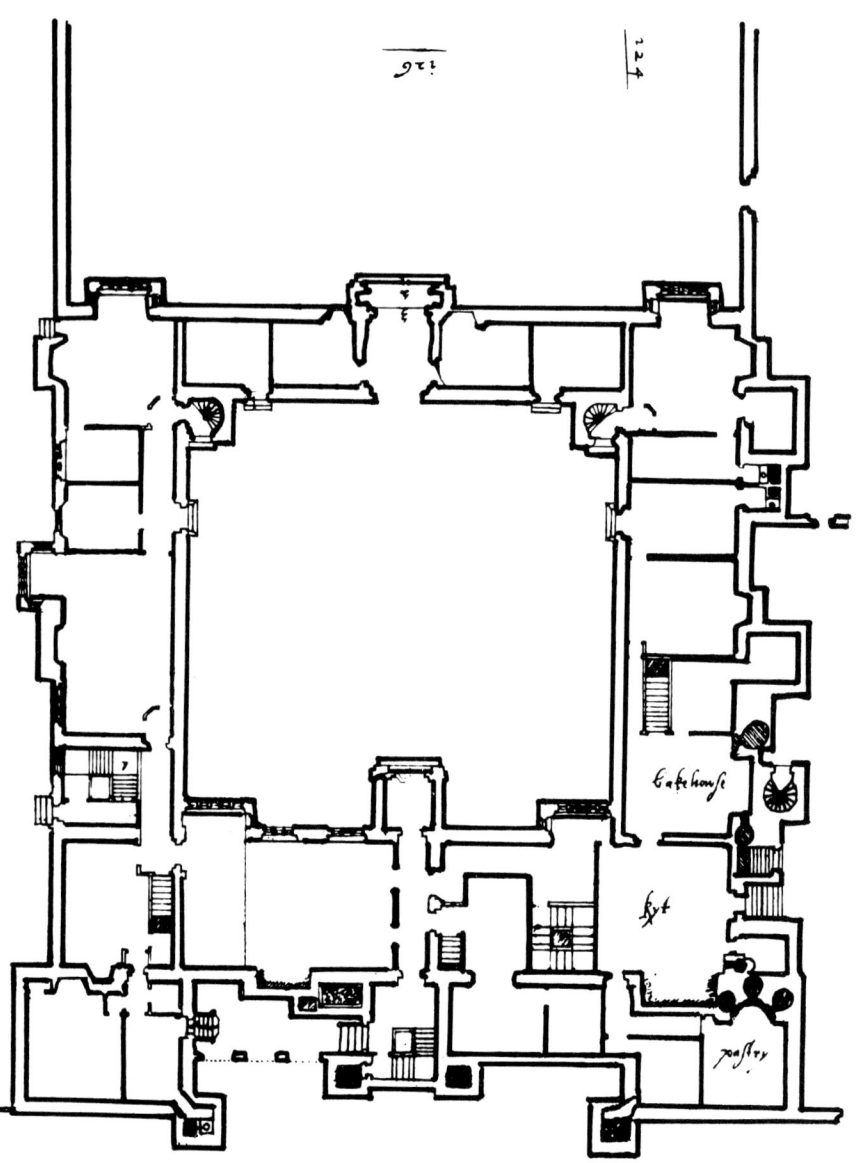

Melford Hall: Thorpe's plan of c. 1615 showing the enlarged West Front incorporating the Gatehouse, Cordell's East Porch and the Eastern Gatehouse demolished c. 1730–40.

Melford Hall: Cordell's Porch of c. 1550. In the French version of the Renaissance style with a pedimented window and round-headed doorway. Note the bold stylised version of the fan motif forming a gable.

Melford Hall: N.E. Turret. Note the Renaissance fan motif on the dome, the square windows of the lantern and the blocked doorway which gave access to the parapet of the demolished East Wing.

Jacobean Extension of c. 1615

Evidence supporting the fact that the three-storied wings are a later addition has been found inside the house where the old external walls have been discovered following the removal of plaster. These walls contain considerable remains of a painted diaper pattern and they appear at both ends of the house at the western end of the long wings. Painted diaper work is most unusual, as a rule the effect was created by using two-toned bricks as at Layer Marney, Hadleigh Deanery, and many other places. It was revived in the nineteenth century and can be seen on the old school at the foot of the Green.

The west front was enlarged for Sir John Savage and the first document we have concerning the work is a plan by John Thorpe in the Sir John Soane's Museum in London. Thorpe was a surveyor and what we would now call an architect although the term was not in general use during his lifetime. He lived 1563—1655 and his name is familiar to us through his collection of drawings and plans of the period. Most of them are from surveys he carried out and are not necessarily his own designs but it is accepted that he was involved with various extensions and alterations. His plan of Melford Hall is undated and it shows the ground floor with the west wings missing from Pierse's drawing of 1613. As Sir John Savage had engaged Pierse in that year to carry out a survey we must assume that Thorpe's plan is for proposed extensions. Whether he was actively involved in the construction has still to be decided but we know from a letter written from Melford Hall in 1619 that the work was completed. It is also obvious from the plan that the early Tudor gatehouse was retained and adapted as the central feature of the new west front.

In 1613 Melford Hall was still very much a late medieval house and it lacked an essential feature of all great Elizabethan and Jacobean houses — a Long Gallery. The extensions were commissioned to make good this defect although Thorpe's plan does not make this clear. However, Sir William Parker in his HISTORY OF LONG MELFORD, published in 1873, quite clearly states:

"... where the first floor west bedrooms are now was originally a long wide open gallery, the principal bedrooms being then small in number."

The west front is therefore a mixture of three distinct periods with the centre and the four turrets being original work of c. 1520. The three-storied wings are c. 1615 and their construction entailed the removal of part of the gatehouse facade. When the outer turrets were incorporated within the new wings the gatehouse effect was lost at a stroke. The centre no longer served as an entrance and was adapted to accommodate an open well staircase giving access to the gallery which occupied three quarters of the width of the new front on the first floor. Another feature typical of Thorpe and shown on his plan was an open loggia which filled the recess formed by the northern turrets. Recent renovations revealed traces of the steps leading down to it. Finally the connecting walls between the centre and the wings were reconstructed in 1813 as we have said before.

Firebrace Alterations 1730–40

The alterations carried out for Sir Cordell Firebrace were intended to create an eighteenth century mansion within the existing shell and we must be thankful that he ignored the current trend of rebuilding from scratch. The first and major casualty was the removal of the eastern gatehouse wing resulting in the loss of much historic architectural evidence and confusing historians ever since. A smaller ornamental gatehouse further east was also removed. The bay windows at the ends of the wings were taken down and replaced with tripartite windows and all the others were sashed. There is a print by Clarke of Melford which shows all this including sash windows to the upper floor of the main Hall block. They were inserted to give a uniform effect but nineteenth century photographs show that the top half were in fact dummies and only the lower sections were functional. Internally many of the rooms were decorated in the Rococo style but little of this has survived.

Hopper's Alterations of 1813–15

The identify of Hopper as the architect responsible for the early nineteenth century alterations has only recently come to light and is fully described in the essay by Gervase Jackson-Stops "Thomas Hopper at Melford and Erdigg" (National Trust Studies 1981). Hopper was an architect employed by the Prince Regent for work on Carlton House in London and was subsequently much sought after by the gentry to adapt and transform their country houses. He was employed at Melford Hall by Sir William Parker, 7th Baronet, who had inherited the estate on the death of his father in 1812. He performed a major reconstruction of the interior of the Hall block and west front

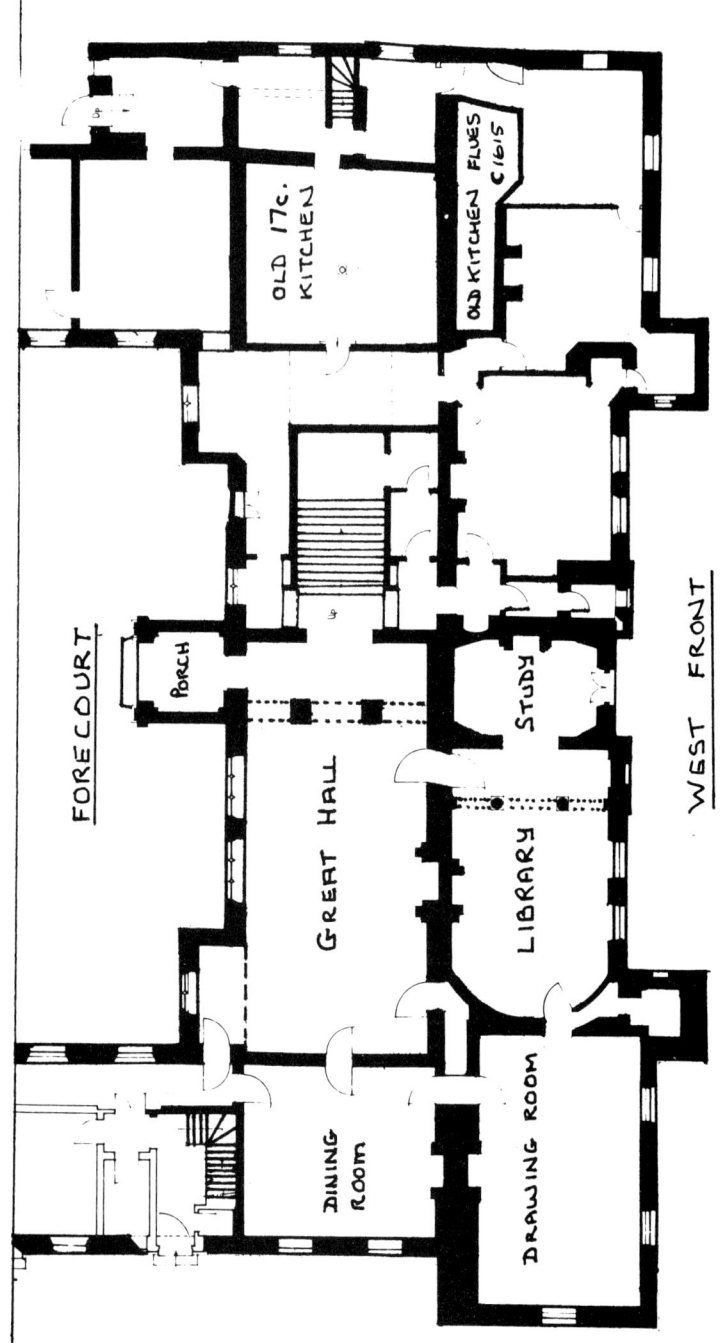

Melford Hall: West Front as altered by Hopper in 1813–15 and as it remains today.

and at the same time replaced Firebrace's tripartite windows at the ends of the wings with the mullioned and transomed versions which still exist. They are shown on a print by T. Higham dated 1818.

The Great Hall has always been two storied with a retainers' gallery above. Recent investigations have shown that this gallery, which is just one long attic, was reconstructed by Hopper when he raised the Hall ceiling and later we shall see why. As we have already learned the principal bedrooms were few in number and to remedy this defect a new range was constructed within the Long Gallery in the west front. The staircase giving access to the gallery was removed and further necessary space was provided by moving the recessed walls forward a few feet. The space occupied by the staircase and the open loggia was utilised to form a new and beautiful library.

The main staircase at Melford Hall was situated in the old serving chamber behind the Screens' Passage, this was taken down and replaced by another which is both audacious and grand. Hopper was to return to Melford Hall in 1840 to work on the north wing for Sir Hyde Parker, 8th Baronet. Because of a serious fire in 1942 while under military occupation none of that work has survived.

The House Today

Having established the evolution of this remarkable house we must now see how much of each period has survived. The approach to the mansion is from the Green through the turreted gateway shown on Clarke's print before 1818 although the lodges were built from designs by Col. Rushbrooke in 1838. The carriageway leads to the forecourt on the east side where the only evidence of the demolished east gatehouse are the blocked doorways which gave access to the parapet. Apart from some obvious signs of restoration the walls surrounding the forecourt belong to the Abbot's house of c. 1520 and that includes the turrets. It should be noted that the parapets are not battlemented. The windows of the Great Hall to the right of the porch were inserted by Sir William Hyde Parker, 9th Baronet, in 1867. They replace the sashed windows from the eighteenth century and may be a fairly accurate representation of the original fenestration.

Interior

The rooms open to the public are all located in the central block and west front. Entrance is through Cordell's handsome porch of c. 1550 with its vaulted ceiling. We find ourselves in the Screens' Passage which before Cordell's time was also approached from the opposite side. The screen has been replaced with a pair of plain Tuscan columns. On our left is the Grand Staircase and on the right the Great Hall, all constructed within the shell of the Abbot's house but in its details mainly 1813. The Jacobean panels and linenfold doors are later additions coeval with the windows of 1867.

Hopper's architectural details are very restrained and it is evident that Sir William Parker had instructed him to create a grand entrance hall in the classic style with tactful reference to its historic past. That he succeeded so well is a tribute to his adaptability when confronted with such a task but what we see is also a tribute to the impeccable taste of his client which becomes more obvious as we progress.

The sheer size of the room is medieval in scale and must surely represent that of the Abbot's original Hall. The great fireplace which dominates the room is clearly based on the eighteenth century style of William Kent and so are the door surrounds. Half way up the wall is a scroll type frieze and between that and the ceiling is a series of grisaille paintings of classical mythological subjects but the artist has not been identified. Whether they were especially commissioned for this room or have been utilised from elsewhere is a matter which deserves fuller investigation. They are set within plaster frames which match the upper window surrounds and their positioning was responsible for the ceiling being raised by Hopper. There is a good collection of stained glass from several periods and it was all assembled by Sir William Hyde Parker, 9th Baronet, in 1867. When he inserted the Jacobean panels and the linenfold doors he merely heightened the illusion already created by Hopper.

With the staircase there is no such restraint or pretence for it is grand, audacious and thoroughly Greek in the French Neo-Classic style. The plain columns which replaced the screen are a prelude to what follows. The stairs rise in one broad sweep with an intermediate landing between plain solid walls. At the top a narrow landing or gallery runs back towards us on either side and it carries a colonnade of plain unfluted Ionic columns supporting a beautiful curved and coffered ceiling.

Melford Hall: The Grand Staircase by Hopper in the French Neo-Classic Style of c. 1813—15. A cascade of stairs with an intermediate landing between plain solid walls. At the top a colonnade supporting the curved and coffered ceiling.

Melford Hall: The Garden House or Gazebo. The Elizabethans called them Banquet Houses. A rare and delightful building c. 1550. The canopy originally covered the entire staircase with the aid of additional columns. The windows were sashed in 1730–40.

Melford Hall: The Garden House. The upper room as adapted in the middle eighteenth century. It has lovely views of The Green, Hall Street, and the gardens.

Across the Hall from the staircase is a doorway leading into the north wing and the Hyde Parker Room. This has modern decor because it was severely damaged in the fire of 1942. Prior to that it had been decorated in the Rococo style of 1740 but from that only the fireplace has survived. This room marks the western extremity of the Abbot's house on this side and it leads into the Drawing Room which has retained its decoration of 1740 but is housed within the Jacobean extension of c. 1615. A really beautiful room with a stunning Rococo fireplace, it has scroll brackets and a pedimented mantlepiece, the finest in the house and one wonders how much has been lost from this period. Other features of 1740 are the pretty dentil cornice of the ceiling and the panel framing of the walls.

A doorway on our left once gave access to the open loggia but now leads into Hopper's Regency Library. The door forms part of an apsed wall to the Library lined with the most exquisite bookcases and the dado surrounding the room is of matching marquetry. At the opposite end is a pair of scagliola columns with a narrow passage behind and then a broad arch leading into the octagonal study. This all forms part of the Library but is constructed within the gatehouse entrance of Abbot Reeve's house. There are beautiful Anthemion friezes to the ceiling cornices and two handsome fireplaces. The furniture is exceptionally fine, much of it apparently designed by Hopper, and is fully described in the N.T. guidebook. A door between the two sections of the Library will bring us back to the Great Hall.

Now we can ascend the Grand Staircase and we have a compulsion to do so with as much dignity as possible. At the top is a broad arch leading into the Boudoir, a room created for Firebrace in the eighteenth century but somewhat altered since. The archway is by Hopper and is an integral part of the Grand Staircase Ensemble but the window is tripartite and similar to those inserted by Firebrace at the ends of the wings and since replaced by Hopper. This room marks the western extremity of the Abbot's house on this side, the wall on our right being an original external wall where diaper decoration has been discovered on what was its outer face.

The narrow landing on the east of the staircase has a stained glass window depicting Queen Elizabeth I which dates from the nineteenth century. The opposite or western landing leads to a doorway where we take a sharp left and right into a corridor lit by skylights. On our right is the bare upper wall of the Abbot's Great Hall but the corridor and the bedrooms on our left fill the space occupied by the Jacobean Long Gallery. The northern-most bedroom did not form part of it but was probably a State Bedroom or Presence Chamber leading off. The Gallery extended from this bedroom to the southern extremity where it ended with a large window, since blocked, and an observation balcony. It must have been very impressive with wainscot walls and richly plastered ceiling. To this day the windows have a western view of open countryside.

The Grounds

They are beautifully maintained with lawns and beds close to the house while parkland stretches away into the distance. On the west side is Cordell's long Tudor brick wall which separates the garden from the moat on the other side and it terminates at a delightful garden house or gazebo, the Elizabethans called them banquet houses. It is two storied and octagonal with eight pinnacled gables constructed with the same beautifully toned red brick of the house. On the garden side there are windows on both levels which are square headed and sashed. A flight of steps leads up to a porch or canopy supported on fluted columns. There is some evidence that the entire staircase was also covered with the help of additional columns. Inside, the upper room has panelled walls and a delightful little eighteenth century fireplace. A lovely place to retreat to, rare and perfect, well worth a visit to Melford for this alone.

The moat ran at right angles to the garden house on the north side according to a survey map of 1735 but the eastern section has since been filled in. It ran southwards beyond the fishponds and then joined up with the mill stream which formed its southern side. This is an unusually extensive moated enclosure and it reflects the importance of the site. It is very close to the junction of two Roman roads and, though it may sound a little fanciful, its origins may well go back beyond the Saxon manor.

James Howell's Letter

James Howell was engaged by Sir John Savage as a companion for his two sons to accompany them on a trip abroad, although in due course the man withdrew when he discovered they were being raised as Catholics. During his short stay at Melford Hall he wrote the following letter to his friend Daniel Caldwell of Sheriff in Essex. Apart from giving us a description of a well-run household, the letter confirms that the Gallery was completed and in use by 1619.

"   May 20, 1619

To Dan. Caldwell Esq., from the Lord Savage's house in Long Melford.

My Dear Dan,
Though considering my former condition in life I may now be called a countryman, yet you cannot call me a rustic (as you imply in your letter) so long as I live in so civil and noble a family, so long as I lodge in so vertuous and regular a house as any I believe in the land, both for economical government and for choice company: for I never saw yet such a dainty race of children in all my life together: I never saw yet such an orderly and punctuall attendance of servants, nor a great house so neatly kept. Here one shall see nor dog nor cat, nor cage, to cause any nastiness within the body of the house. The Kitchin and gutters and other offices of noise and drudgery are at the fag end: There is a back gate for the beggars and meaner sort of swains to come in at. The stables butt upon the park, which for a chearfull rising ground, for groves and browsing ground for the deer, and for rivulets of water may compare with any for its bigness, in the whole land. It is opposite to the front of the great house from whence from the gallery one may see much of the game when they are hunting.

Now, for the gardening and costly choice flowers, for ponds, for stately large walks, green and gravelly, for orchards, and choice fruits of all sorts, there are few the like in England. There you have your Bon Christien Pear and Bergamott in perfection —

your Muscadell grapes in such plentie that there are some bottles of wine sent every year to the King; and one Mr Daniell, a worthy gentleman hard by, who hath been long abroad, makes good store in his vintage. Truly this house of Long Melford, tho it be not so great, yet it is so well compacted and contrived with such dainty conveniences every way, that if you saw the landskip of it, you would be mightily taken with it, and it would serve for a choice pattern to build and contrive a house by. If you come this summer to your Mannor of Sherriff in Essex, you will not be far off hence, and if your occasions will permit, it will be worth your coming hither.
    Yours,
      James Howell.   "

Until now, it has been assumed that the reference to a Gallery in this letter meant the roof-top of the demolished east wing as it faced the park. To add to the confusion Sir William Parker's HISTORY OF LONG MELFORD contains an illustration with a reconstruction of the house showing a suspended bridge between the turrets. He based his reconstruction on the Pierse drawing (and also left out the West Front) but there is no evidence that such a bridge ever existed. When the new West Front was constructed it became the back of the house, Cordell's porch was the main entrance just as it is today. As we have already explained, the rooms occupying the Gallery space still have views over open fields and this is where Howell watched the hunt.

Abbot John Reeve

The Abbot has been credited with the bulk of the Tudor construction on stylistic evidence and the original plan of the Hall and the undeniable fact that there is not a single record to substantiate the attribution to Cordell. We do, however, have evidence that the Abbot took an unusual interest in his Manor houses and Granges. We know for certain that he rebuilt Little Horringer Hall but his mania for building is confirmed in the report on him from the Commissioner for the Suppression of Religious Houses:—

". . . as for the Abbot, we find nothing to sospect as touching his living, but it was detected that he laye moche forth in his granges: that he delited moche in

playing at dice and cardes, and therein spent moche
money, and in building for his pleasure. . ."

This mania, which he shared with that other Suffolk contemporary and prelate Cardinal Wolsey, illustrates the great wealth which could be available for such projects through the church. In Suffolk Archdeacon Pykenham had built minor palaces at Ipswich and Hadleigh before he died in 1497 and although only the Gatehouses have survived, that at Hadleigh being spectacular, they indicate quite clearly the high standard of living these churchmen enjoyed.

The Renaissance Style in Suffolk

The revival of the classic style of Greece and Rome came to full flower in Italy during the fifteenth century and spread through to France and the rest of the continent, each country having its own variations. It was late coming to England and it has always been accepted that the first showing was with the tomb of Henry VII in Westminster Abbey. Pietro Torrigiano was the sculptor and it was completed in 1512. Two years later Wolsey began work on Hampton Court, a palace built around two great courtyards in the late medieval English style.

Hampton Court's Renaissance details are few and purely decorative but they are some of the first to appear on a domestic building in England. Chief of them is the series of terracotta roundels of Roman emperors by Giovanni de Maiano which decorate a gatehouse. It has been claimed that they are the first terracotta ornament to be seen in England. The Great Hall has an impressive hammer-beam roof, very English but with some Renaissance detail this time carved by an Englishman, Richard Rydge. In a room known as Wolsey's closet is a rich ceiling with moulded ribs forming interlaced geometric forms which is again claimed to be the earliest of its type in the country.

Just three miles from Melford, at St. Gregory's church in Sudbury, there are terracotta gargoyles and roof bosses in the north aisle. The bosses are without Gothic detail, one of them displays a wreath of laurels and another depicts a hound. The chancel of the same church has a flat ceiling with a pattern of interlaced hexagons and squares formed by moulded ribs. Both terracotta ornament and ceiling pre-date Hampton Court by thirty years.

At Layer Marney Tower, about twenty five miles from Melford, are the impressive remains of a manor house never completed but contemporary with Melford and Hampton Court.

The surviving gatehouse and adjoining wing have giant windows of terracotta covered with Renaissance detail. The parapets of the gatehouse are of the same material with a battlemented effect created by fan shapes similar to the lunettes on the Melford turrets. In spite of all this there are some fifty smaller windows on the south front and a further fourteen on the north side of a Gothic form with the late Perpendicular or Tudor depressed arch. There is also much diaper patterning created with different coloured bricks.

Similar terracotta windows to Layer Marney appear in Suffolk at Shrubland Old Hall near Ipswich and in the churches of Barham, Barking and Henley. Pevsner has suggested that they may well be formed from the same moulds, presumably by the same workmen. At Sutton Place in Surrey, which was built by Sir Richard Weston in 1520, is another display of terracotta ornament.

Hengrave Hall, near Bury St. Edmunds, is another courtyard house begun in 1525 and completed in 1538. The Renaissance features here are again purely decorative and they take the form of putti or cherubs supporting armorial shields above the gatehouse entrance. All other decoration at Hengrave is essentially Gothic but there is one significant feature concerning the plan of the house which is not. A corridor runs three sides round the centre court, this was clearly based on the plan of a Roman Villa and its revival at this early date is of great interest.

Apart from the plan at Hengrave all the foregoing refers to Renaissance decorative detail only and this is where we come to the important significance of Melford Hall. The six turrets in all their height are completely devoid of Gothic ornament or detail. The windows are square and not arched and the absence of battlements compensated for by the domes with their fan-shaped lunettes all point to a first real break from the Gothic style in England. The great tragedy is that none of the original windows have survived in other parts of the house although work on the south wing in 1974 revealed that they had straight heads with a mullion and transom. The demolished east wing would have told us more but Pierse's drawing, taken from the south, does not give sufficient detail. When Henry VIII underwent his breach with Rome it effectively checked the early Renaissance movement in England. English architecture became influenced by the Dutch, French and German versions rather than the Italian until the arrival of Inigo Jones in the seventeenth century.

Melford Place: The home of the Martyn family from the late fourteenth century until 1765. The south wing containing a private chapel is all that remains from their house c. 1525.

Melford Place: Interior of the chapel showing the outline of the late Perpendicular east window with Dr. Westropp's later window inserted.

MELFORD PLACE

This was the third major house in the village and was the home of the Martyn family from the late fourteenth century until 1765. It is situated at the southern end of the main street on the right hand side facing Chapel Green. Richard Martyn, the founder of the Melford family, was a wealthy wool merchant from Dorset. His family were deeply religious and after the Reformation remained staunch Catholics in spite of deprivations, fines, and restrictions on their movements. Their constancy was shared by the Waldegraves at nearby Borley to whom they were related by marriage.

Prior to the Reformation Richard's son Laurence, who died in 1460, had built a small chapel on the south side of the church where he was buried. It was rebuilt by his sons Roger and Richard II whose names appear on the parapet inscriptions. The family also took an active interest in the small chapel of St. James which stood on the Green opposite their house.

Melford Place began its existence as a timber-framed hall with cross-wings and as the family and their fortunes increased so the house was enlarged and improved, although the process was reversed in the late seventeenth century. It was Roger II, who died in 1542, who was responsible for certain enlargements which included a brick built south wing containing a chapel. His eldest son and heir, Richard III (died 1572) married a daughter of the Eden family from Sudbury Priory. This alliance was of some significance because Thomas Eden, Clerk of the Star Chamber, was married to Grissell Waldegrave whose father was a member of Queen Mary's household and of course a very firm Catholic. The Edens, however, were to become one of the foremost Puritan families in East Anglia. With this marriage therefore the Martyns gained a foot in each camp.

Roger III (b. 1526 d. 1615) inherited the house and he was the man who left a vivid account of the church before the Reformation. He was offered a position as Secretary of State by Queen Mary but refused it because he preferred a simple life in his native village. It was his cousin Roger IV who lived in London and became Sheriff of that city in 1559 and Lord Mayor in 1567–8, which effectively demonstrates the often overlooked leniency and toleration of the first ten years of Elizabeth's reign.

It was the infamous Papal Bull "Regnans in Excelsis" of 1570, which declared the Queen a heretic, a bastard, and excommunicate, that finally put the cat among the pigeons. With this Bull the Pope declared that all Englishmen were released from their allegiance to Queen Elizabeth and were expected to rebel. The Martyns, like all other Catholics, were faced with a cruel dilemma, loyalty to their Queen and State or obedience to the Pope and their Church. They chose to be loyal to their sovereign and somehow managed to remain Catholics and steer a delicate middle course.

Sir Roger Martyn, third Baronet, who died in 1672 was the last member of the family to reside here and after his death the property was sold to a Mr. Stephen Oliver, Gent. of London. It later came into the possession of a Miss Gardiner who married into the Spalding family but by 1790 she was a widow and remarried, this time to Dr. Westropp who lived in Hall Street and from whom the present owner is descended.

Melford Place, in spite of various structural alterations, retained its basic 'H' plan until the late eighteenth century. A drawing of the house appears on a survey plan drawn up for Stephen Oliver and it shows a central block with a row of five casement windows on the upper floor, a central doorcase flanked by a pair of casements on either side and two long wings. It is apparent that the house was remodelled in the seventeenth century. The forecourt was quite deep and there can be little doubt that in its original form it was closed in on the east side with a brick wall pierced by an archway.

At some time during the eighteenth century the north wing was destroyed and the south wing, which contained the Chapel, was divided horizontally, its tudor brick windows blocked and the outer walls rendered. Dr. Westropp refronted and remodelled the main block which reduced the depth of the forecourt considerably. He moved the entrance to the south side where it remains today and restored the chapel to its full height, partially unblocked the east window and brought back some panels which had been removed to the church to form a pew in the Martyn Chapel.

There are a few external features which give some idea of the true age of the Chapel and they are all to be found on the north wall. From the street is clearly visible a blocked Tudor brick window which was, because of its position, obviously meant to light a Rood or crucifix. From the garden can be seen another blocked window on a lower level and a section of the wall which has been exposed to reveal a diaper pattern of two-toned bricks.

Somehow we do not expect to find much of interest with regard to the interior and there is nothing to prepare one for the very pleasant shock when passing over the threshold. The chapel is open from floor to roof and now forms an impressive reception room. The extraordinary wealth of timber from the staircase, gallery, fireplace, wainscot, and above all the roof is almost overwhelming. They are, of course, from various periods but blend together to form a most remarkable and tasteful ensemble.

The complete shell of the sixteenth century chapel has survived although the south wall has been pierced with later fenestration. The eye is drawn instantly to the east end where the moulding of the giant window with its late Perpendicular arch is fully exposed. Dr. Westropp's straight-headed mullioned and transomed window is set within the framework. High up on the left is the blocked window we saw from outside. Above all this is the splendid roof which runs the full length of the chapel.

Because of the relatively narrow width of the building, the roof is of the simplest double-frame construction with wall plates projecting to form a cornice. At each end is a cambered tie-beam supporting the ridge beam. The closely spaced rafters are moulded and slope down from the ridge to the wall plate where they curve sharply, thereby forming a shallow arch span. The moulded profile of each rafter is picked out in a shade of red but the space between them is boarded and coloured blue. There is oak leaf carving of a very high standard all along the wall plates and ridge beam. The eastern tie-beam is carved with a splendid dragon amongst foliage and there is more of the same lush carving on the western counterpart. At the centre of the ridge beam is a carved representation of a 'Woodwose' or Green Man. This beautiful roof dating from the first quarter of the sixteenth century is also remarkable for the fact that there is not a single religious motif of any kind.

Next in chronological order and aesthetic appeal is the series of Renaissance panels set within the wainscot. Several of them are portrait profiles within roundels and there are others combining foliage and strapwork. They probably date from 1530–40 and appear to be Dutch or Flemish. It is most unlikely that the portraits represent members of the Martyn family and it is worth noting that two such panels can be seen at All Saints

Melford Place: The Chapel roof with curved and moulded rafters sloping from the carved ridge beam to the decorated wall plates.

Melford Place: The Chapel. Seventeenth century gallery at the west end. The last fixture to be installed by the Martyn family.

Vicarage in Sudbury and they were moved there from Sir Edward Waldegrave's house which stood nearby. A similar series of high quality was moved from Sir Anthony Wingfield's house in Tacket Street, Ipswich to Christchurch Mansion where they now form a distinguished feature of that most interesting museum. Included in the Melford Place series are the two panels depicting the arms of Martyn and Eden. There are also some earlier panels of the linenfold type.

The fireplace and overmantle is set in the centre of the north wall and is not an original feature of the Chapel. It was probably placed here in the early seventeenth century and is constructed from a mixture of late Tudor and early Jacobean woodwork. The overmantle is crowned with a representation of the Prince of Wales' feathers.

At the western end of the Chapel and immediately above the wainscot is a gallery or balcony with a balustrade front from the seventeenth century. Apparently it was the last fixture to be installed by the Martyns. The balusters are beautifully carved and there is a good solid top rail. At the back of the gallery is a door of the same period set within some interesting sixteenth century panels rather like the base of a Rood Screen and they may well have originally served that purpose.

The staircase is not strictly part of the Chapel but it has a handsome balustrade coeval with the gallery to which it gives access. Mr. C. Westropp Cutler, the present owner, told me how the dreadful fire of 1967 destroyed the main block and reached the top of this staircase to consume a grandfather clock which stood on the landing. The flames were only inches away from the Chapel and its escape can only be regarded as a miracle.

As Catholics in a Puritan stronghold, the Martyn family were spared much local persecution because they were a well established and much liked family with a reputation for generosity. The alliance with the Eden family, so proudly proclaimed on the wainscot, probably helped matters considerably as well. There was nothing wrong with having a domestic chapel, indeed family prayers were encouraged, but saying Mass and worshiping images was strictly forbidden. As we have noticed already the Chapel is devoid of religious ornament which points to caution but no doubt an image or two was concealed about the house. After the religious turmoil and the Civil War, Sir Roger Martyn, then aged twenty seven, was created a Baronet in recognition of his family's loyalty to the Crown throughout their most difficult times. In spite of their

Melford Place: The Chapel: Some of the Renaissance panels which line the chapel walls. They were removed to the church in the eighteenth century when the chapel was divided but brought back by Dr. Westropp in the nineteenth century. Probably Dutch or Flemish.

contribution to the rebuilding of the church before all those troubles began their most significant memorial at Melford must surely be this lovely private Chapel where they worshiped with their servants down the centuries.

Melford Place is a private residence and not open to the public and I am most grateful to the owners for allowing me access for the purposes of this book.

THE MINOR BUILDINGS

After the splendours of the church and the Tudor halls the remaining buildings must come under this heading but only in a comparative sense. Apart from their obvious contribution to the attractions of Melford they are in themselves important links with the village's historic past. Many of them are intrinsically sixteenth century but later modifications tend to disguise the fact. You will not find vast areas of exposed timber as at nearby Lavenham where the uncovering of beams has been carried to excess. At Melford they have been wise to let well alone, consequently leaving a fascinating array of facades representing all architectural periods down the centuries. The clue to a building's true age can usually be found in the roof levels and by studying them a surprising number of Hall-type houses are revealed, though they have frequently been sub-divided. Obviously some of the minor buildings are more important than others but the loss of any of them would be tragic.

Suffolk, at least this corner of it, has no building stone, therefore after timber, we have brick of which there is an abundance. It can be seen in a full range of subtle tones from the Tudor red to the eighteenth and nineteenth century white or grey. Several of the later timber-framed houses are plastered but there is a dearth of pargeting which is surprising. Georgian pedimented doorcases and Venetian windows abound but often the rooms behind are Tudor or Jacobean. There are contributions from the Victorian era but none of it ugly, in fact one of the pleasures at the foot of the Green is the old school of 1860 with its turret and diapered brick walls tactfully grouped to complement the visual splendours surrounding it. Victorian also is the red brick mass of Montgomery House, formerly the Rectory, tactfully recessed by the church gate. It was built in 1870 and for that date is remarkably restrained in a late Elizabethan style.

*Two of the houses flanking the Green.
Ely House (below) is a typical hybrid house.
Late Georgian stuccoed facade with earlier timber framed interior.*

Tact is a virtue not usually associated with the Victorians but they exercised it at Melford to an unprecedented degree.

If any building has caused controversy with regard to tact it is The Hospital of the Undivided Trinity which is positioned at the top of the Green and immediately in front of the church. It was founded by William Cordell in 1573 for twelve poor men and two servants and occupies the site of a previous almshouse which certainly existed in 1442. The land on which it stands formed part of Monks Manor which was leased to the Clopton family for many years but was subsequently granted to Cordell at the dissolution of the monasteries. The original building was single storied with almshouses forming three sides of a quadrangle and a great hall on the fourth. A that time it did not obscure the church so we can discount the theory that it was deliberately sited to spite the Cloptons. We have to remember that other buildings stood alongside before the Hospital was built. Cordell was more than generous to his twelve poor men or Melford for he gave them a home on a site which commands the finest view in the village and one of the most coveted in East Anglia. The Green was the centre of activity in Melford and the Hospital inmates were made to feel part of the community. The building was completely reconstructed from the basement level in 1847 so the only original parts visible to the eye are the boundary walls with the delightful and slightly pompous stone gateway. It says much for the designer of the nineteenth century building that it is often mistaken for the real thing and that is because in all its details they are correct for the early Tudor style it emulates. There is a centre block of five bays flanked by two short projecting wings all with battlemented parapets. The wings are of one bay with gables and pinnacles and they have battlemented bay windows on the ground floor. The centre block has as its accents a pretty cupola with a weather vane and a central bay window on the first floor. Tudor-type chimneys abound, mainly in pairs, and the almshouses at the rear still form three sides of a quadrangle but at a lower level. The windows throughout are of the Tudor type with arched lights and lattice glazing.

The remaining buildings flanking the Green are from various periods and most pleasing to the eye. Flanking the Hospital at the approach to the church is a timber-framed but plastered group of five cottages. They seem to date from the late seventeenth century but the later fenestration has given

Gateways on The Green: The restored entrance to Cordell's almshouses which form the Hospital of the Holy and Undivided Trinity founded in 1573.

Gateways on The Green: The entrance gateway to Melford Hall designed to compliment the Tudor House. The archway early nineteenth century but the lodges a little later.

The Hospital of the Holy and undivided Trinity: Often accepted as an original Tudor building but reconstructed from the basement level in 1847. The garden wall was originally built in 1633 and has been carefully restored in recent years.

*Melford Green:
A very pleasant run of
houses on the west side.
Above: late 17C row
of modest cottages.
Below: late 18C
reminiscent of
a doll's house.*

Melford Green: Two more hybrid houses with interesting and attractive facades. Falkland House (below) is probably the oldest on the Green and began its life as a tavern in the 16th century.

them an eighteenth century appearance. Each cottage has a canted bay window on the ground foor only, which makes them especially attractive. A few doors down is Ely House, typical of many in Melford with a late Georgian front concealing a timber-framed rear. The facade of three bays with a parapet and pillared porch is stuccoed. The centre bay is narrow but the outer bays have broad tripartite sashed windows on both floors. Apart from its honest and well proportioned facade there is nothing particularly special about this house but we mention it because it is typical, not only of Melford, but of Suffolk. Again and again we shall come across the hybrid house, sometimes it will have a Georgian brick front, sometimes Victorian, sometimes believe it or not a mock Tudor facade, but at its core is always the good old Suffolk timber frame.

On the corner of Westgate Street is the three-storied Black Lion Inn, built in 1840 to replace its seventeenth century predecessor. Obviously positioned to attract the travellers on the old Roman road from Clare and beyond but at its busiest during the annual horse fair which was held on the Green. Horse dealers came to it from all over England and they included many gypsies. George Borrow, the writer and friend of gypsies, prize-fighters, horse dealers and their like, knew it well and mentioned Melford in 'Lavengro'. The fair is still held at Whitsuntide but is now merely a fun-fair, which is a pity. It must be one of the oldest still surviving in England. The site of the medieval fair is marked by the base of a cross, destroyed in 1615, which can be seen close to Falkland House.

Falkland House stands a few yards south of Westgate Street and is probably the oldest house flanking the Green on this side, it is certainly the most interesting. The superstructure and the main chimney stack date from the middle sixteenth century, the dormered roof is a century later and the windows were inserted in the eighteenth century. It began life as The Eight Bells Inn (but sometimes called the Eight Ringers) and later became The White Lion. Timber-framed and plastered of three broad bays, that on the right being a two-storied canted bay, the others double sashed on the upper floor. It had a very extensive garden at the rear, part of which backed on to Westgate Street where fragments of a serpentine wall still stand. These walls are usually of the eighteenth century and seem to be mainly confined to East Anglia; Melford has six examples. They were designed to provide sheltered bays for peach trees etc. as well as providing a wall of considerable strength with the minimum quantity of bricks. Another attractive feature is the shallow bow shape of the front garden railings.

Further down is gabled Sloane Cottage, much redone in the early nineteenth century with shallow Regency type oriels on the upper floor and an interesting doorcase. Immediately alongside are two broad early nineteenth century houses of which the second is the finest with a recessed two bay centre flanked by single broad bays. All the windows have Tudor-type hood moulds. Gentle bowed garden railings are in front of the carriage sweep as at Falkland House. The remaining houses are a very pleasant mixture of styles culminating with a row of late seventeenth century cottages with dormers.

In the centre of the Green, close to the main road, is the gabled and pinnacled Tudor brick conduit-house constructed over a spring-fed well which supplied water for the villagers and a piped supply for Melford Hall. it was built in the sixteenth century, quite possibly by the Abbot, and is one of a pair. The other stood further up the Green towards the church but being that much closer to the burial ground the water must have been of doubtful purity.

On the east side of the Green, across the busy main road, is the clay pit which provided the material for the bricks of Melford Hall and the Hospital. It was the property of the Lord of the Manor but villagers were allowed to extract clay for themselves over the centuries. The thatched cottage was built in the seventeenth century and it has an unrivalled view of the church.

Further down on the same side is the turreted gatehouse of Melford Hall with the Garden House and Cordell's boundary wall reflected in the moat and an impressive display of topiary. The footpath takes us over the Chad Brook with the mill house on our right. This is a late seventeenth century timber-framed house with twin gables facing south towards Hall Street. For a few years before his death it was the home of the poet Edmund Blunden who was buried in the churchyard in 1974. The weatherboarded mill which stood behind the house and was such a picturesque feature of Melford has been demolished. From the footbridge we can see how the mill leat formed the southern boundary of the moat while on the right is a lovely view of the road bridge with trees and meadows beyond, rather unexpected at this point.

We find ourselves at the Little Green with the vaguely Tudor-style Police Station and Courthouse of 1849 now neatly

Little Green: Timber-frame and plaster, Georgian red brick, and 18C weatherboarding. Below: an early 19C grey brick terrace. The doorways become more dignified from left to right as each house progresses from one to three bays in width.

Two views from the footpath by the Mill denied to motorists. Right: The Mill ford which gave the village its name was bridged in 1762. Below: The Renaissance turrets of Melford Hall rising above a fine display of topiary on the banks of the moat.

converted into houses. It faces the site of the vanished stocks, pillory, and ducking stool. Overlooking this part of the Green is a run of houses forming one of the most attractive groups in Melford. In sequence there is timber-framing, Georgian red brick, weatherboarding and early nineteenth century grey brick — once white.

Across the road is the homely but impressive bulk of Brook House, timber-framed but with brick infilling from the nineteenth century. This is the first example we have come across of the medieval Hall-type house and is worth studying because its subsequent development is plainly visible from outside. To start with we must try to ignore the handsome timber porch with its date of 1610. It may look authentic but is in fact constructed from old materials and is one of a pair in Melford, the other is dismantled in an outhouse at Melford Hall.

Brook House is a typical example of a Suffolk merchant's house of c. 1490 and in its original form consisted of a main hall block, single storied, with a northern cross-wing to the right. Interior evidence tells us that the southern cross-wing was added a few years later. The timber frame at that time had an infilling of wattle and daub. The upper floor of the wings were jettied, just as they are today, but there is evidence that it continued along the lane side. The central hall was heated by an open hearth with a louvered vent in the roof to allow the smoke to escape. At some time in the early sixteenth century, probably when the south wing was constructed, the hall was divided horizontally and a chimney inserted, the upper floor then forming the main bed chamber with low walls and high pitched roof. In 1575 it was the home of William Dash, a modest land owner who also leased the mill from Cordell. During his ownership the hall block was raised and its roof reconstructed. By 1613 the house had become the White Hart Inn and the wings were extended at the rear. The last major reconstruction was in the nineteenth century when much of the fenestration was altered and the original infilling was replaced with bricks. The garden wall appears to be of 17C date.

Almost opposite is The Bull Hotel, another merchant's house, but of the long facade fronting Hall Street only the section from Bull Lane to the gable is original. The remainder is an excellent reproduction from our own times. In the early nineteenth century all the timbers were concealed behind a plain brick facade which lasted until 1935. When it was removed some of the timbers had to be replaced and the gable

Brook House: Timber-framed hall-house begun c. 1490 but extended during the next two hundred years. Brick-nogging between the timbers early 19C.

The Bull Hotel: Built for a wealthy wool and cloth merchant c. 1500. Given a brick facade in the early 19th century but removed in 1935.

was added, although the rooms behind are original.

The merchant who built this house was obviously quite wealthy because the quality of the timber and the decorative carving is of a very high standard. It dates from the beginning of the sixteenth century and apart from being a home it also housed a weaving complex and storage rooms. In its original state it was similar to Brook House with gabled cross-wings at either end, the upper floors being jettied along the front and sides. The gables were removed to accommodate the brick facade. However, at The Bull we have stepped one pace forward in the evolution of the timber-framed house because from the start the Hall had an upper floor and chimneys. Apart from that, the medieval Screens' Passage has given way to a sturdily built entrancy lobby.

With the cloth industry drawing to a close towards the end of the century we find that in 1580 it had become an inn. This was the fate of many such houses in Suffolk which has often meant the preservation of them. In 1613 William Drew was the landlord and he obviously ran a very successful business because in 1649 he proudly embellished the entrance with carved doorposts bearing his initials and the date. On the upper brackets he has also cheekily borrowed the fan motif from the turrets of Melford Hall.

The Hall is now a lounge where people gather for afternoon tea beneath its carved and moulded beams and in the winter warm themselves by the huge open fireplace. There is a fascinating carving of a 'Woodwose' or Green Man, a subject often found in Suffolk churches. He stands naked with a girdle of foliage about his loins and a wreath on his head. In his left hand he carries a club, while his right firmly grasps a swan's neck. He is surrounded by more carved foliage.

There is a great deal of exposed timber throughout the house and another giant fireplace in the dining room. Upstairs there are considerable remains of an open gallery, now closed in, which reminds us that this was an important coaching inn on the Norwich—London run during the eighteenth and nineteenth centuries. Throughout that period the inn also boasted an Assembly Room used by the villagers for balls and assemblies as so beautifully described by Jane Austen in 'EMMA'. Today it is one of the foremost hotels in East Anglia with excellent facilities for the tourist and the locals.

HALL STREET

From the Bull Hotel to Melford Place runs the main thoroughfare which has been known as Hall Street since the fifteenth century, if not before. Beyond the Green towards Bury it becomes High Street because it does indeed cross higher ground. At its southernmost point Hall Street forms part of the Roman road from London, therefore its most distant echo is the sound of the legionaries' marching feet. From the eleventh century for five hundred years it formed part of the main pilgrimage route to the shrine of St. Edmund at Bury as well as a trade route to Norwich and Lynne. Along this street came the impressive cavalcade of knights, gentlemen, horsemen and servants which accompanied Elizabeth to Melford Hall as guest of Cordell. A few years later the more comical sight of Will Kemp, one of Shakespear's actors, dancing from London to Norwich, no doubt caused much merriment. In 1641 between two and three thousand angry anti-papists and anti-royalists rampaged along the street in pursuit of the unfortunate Countess Rivers. For two centuries after that turkeys and cattle were driven "on the hoof" from Norfolk to the London markets along this thoroughfare and until the railway forced them out of business it was an important coaching route.

The unusual width emphasises the importance of the street which by the fifteenth century was lined with merchants' halls, tradesmen's premises, shops, inns, and lesser houses, just as it is today. It is now recognised as being one of the most attractive village streets in East Anglia and the buildings are enhanced by groups of trees which appear spasmodically along its length. If anything detracts it is the ever-present motor car which seems to be parked everywhere, especially at the height of the tourist season. There is also a curious reluctance to number several of the houses which has made the task of identifying them more difficult than is necessary. However, these are minor quibbles which must not be allowed to spoil our pleasure.

There is of course an abundance of minor architectural detail of interest, such as Georgian and Regency doorcases, bay windows, cornices, etc., far too many to be listed in detail but most of them are covered in the illustrations. The roof levels are particularly worth studying with brick chimney stacks from the fifteenth and sixteenth centuries appearing frequently as valuable clues above a bewildering assortment of later facades. Each building quietly makes its own contribution so that it is

Hall Street, East Side: Nos. 7, 8 and 9. Behind the late nineteenth century facade is a substantial timber-framed Hall house.

Hall Street, East Side: Blyth House, central hall with dormers added later and gabled cross-wings. c. 1490.

Hall Street as a whole that is memorable. None of the buildings are dramatic or astounding although some are worthy of special attention and they are listed accordingly. Aesthetically Hall Street should be traversed from the south end so that it acts as a prelude to the visual splendours of The Green but as most visitors seem to make straight for the Church and the Halls they miss that extra pleasure. So that we do not get confused en route it must be remembered that Hall Street runs north to south, the Bull is therefore on the east side and that is where we start our journey.

East Side

Cleeve Cottage — Modest but charming, three bays with hood moulds over the ground floor windows which are sashed. This is a late eighteenth century facade but there is a tell-tale chimney with twin octagonal shafts which points to an earlier date — probably middle sixteenth century.

Nos. 7, 8 and 9 — Almost unique in actually being numbered. A broad Victorian front disguising a substantial timber-framed Hall house with projecting cross-wings at the rear. Like the Bull the cross-wings were originally gabled but the roof has been remodelled to accommodate the brick facade. Good chimney stacks.

Denzil Antiques and Brian Watts — Both owners expressed complete ignorance of door numbers. They share one of the oldest and most interesting houses in Hall Street. The antique shop occupies the cross-wing and part of another timber-framed group of a slightly later date. The cross-wing dates from the middle fifteenth century and is constructed with very solid timbers. As it is a shop we have access and the upper floor, which was the solar, is still open to the ridge. There are two rooms and there is evidence that the ridge beam was originally braced. Good fireplace downstairs. Next door was once the hall which was divided horizontally in the middle sixteenth century when the enormous chimney stack was inserted. Nicely moulded chimney beam to the fireplace downstairs and an original timber doorway of c. 1450 which

once gave access to the yard but now leads into a late seventeenth century extension. Upstairs is a good brick open fireplace.
External details: Cross-wing and hall have a nineteenth century brick front, not unattractive. Slight change in roof level shows the extent of late seventeenth century extension. Beautiful chimney stack with four massive octagonal shafts. Nice Victorian shop window, similar to many in Hall Street.

Blyth House No name shown but located opposite the Post Office just past the Victorian three-storied Chestnut Terrace. Under renovation at the time of writing. This is another hall house but more obviously so this time. Central hall and gabled cross-wings all of c. 1490. The hall divided horizontally quite late with the upper floor lit by dormers. Plenty of exposed timber including original doorways, all good quality. Victorian shop windows to the wings with tripartite windows to the upper floors. One can well understand the temptation to remove them and expose the original timbers but so far this house has escaped the 'Lavenham' treatment — but for how long?

Tudor Cottages 1 — 5 A very attractive group, timber-framed behind plaster, some of the timber exposed, especially the brackets supporting the oversailing. Middle sixteenth century in origin. No. 1 has three attractive cantilevered bay windows from the eighteenth century. No. 2 has retained its original Tudor doorway. No. 3 has two very narrow doorcases flanked by two pairs of 'Gothik' windows, early nineteenth century probably. The shutters folded back and decorated with Gothic carving which seems to be earlier. Is it possible that this has been taken from the church?
Several attractive cottages with later fronts before Chestnut House.

Hall Street, East Side: Tudor Cottages c. 1550. Original timber frame covered with 17C plaster, 19C windows for once an added attraction.

Hall Street, East Side: Chestnut House with most elegant facade of grey brick and splendid doorcase. It masks a medieval Hall house with timber frame.

Hall Street, East Side: Lime Cottage with lovely plaster front concealing the timber frame.

Chestnut House	Originally a timber-framed Hall house but now graced with an exquisite late Georgian facade in white (now grey) brick. How one admires the Georgian's expertise and taste when faced with the adaptation of an earlier building. A finely proportioned three bay centre which projects just a few inches flanked by single broad bays representing the cross-wings. Good pedimented Tuscan doorcase centrally placed. Shallow parapet with dentil cornice runs the full width of the house. Very nice simple railings to the shallow garden. Altogether the epitome of late Georgian taste and elegance.
Posting House, Countryman Restaurant and Yeomans	Another sixteenth century Hall house with gabled cross-wings, could possibly date from late fifteenth. Much exposed timber inside, including crown post in the roof of the hall which has of course been divided horizontally. Left hand cross-wing had original solar above with parlour below. Right cross-wing, now Yeomans, may have consisted of domestic offices and workshops in its original state.
Magpie Cottage Lime Cottage	A small cottage, timber-framed but such large timbers which suggests that this is a fragment of a much larger house. The cottage to the left has much lighter timbers which ought not to be exposed. On the right of Magpie is Lime Cottage which has retained its original plaster front and two pretty canted bay windows.
Linden House, Ardleigh, The Laurels, George and Dragon, etc.	Immediately after Lime Cottage begins a run of Victoriana. Linden and Ardleigh are semi-detached houses with almost identical facades of grey brick. They conceal yet another substantial timber-framed house. Next door is the George and Dragon, a nice little pub with early Victorian front but eighteenth century rear. Pleasant little alley alongside with long stretches of red brick garden walls. On the other side of the alley is The Laurels, a monster Victorian villa with a giant square Italianate belvedere. It ought to look completely out of place but somehow doesn't.

Hall Street, East Side: Mansell Hall with an elegant Georgian facade, the finest of its date in Melford, c. 1750.

Hall Street, East Side: Archway Cottage with original doorway which gave access to the Screens' Passage of a central hall c. 1500.

Hall Street, East Side: Corpus Christi or Cadge's House. Behind the 19C facade is an interior of c. 1480 of great interest.

Built by a Mr. C.J.N. Rowe whose Insurance Office stands alongside. Narrow gabled front with an abundance of nineteenth century commercial lettering, in its own way a little gem. Holgate has a good doorcase with reeded columns and straight metope pediment. Next the gabled front of the Old Maltings with its cantilevered hoist, grey brick and remarkably restrained.

Mansel Hall
Back to the restrained elegance of the middle eighteenth century, this time in smouldering red brick. Five bays with broad centre graced with a Venetian window on the upper floor and the finest doorcase in Melford below. Pedimented with plain Doric columns, much fine detail on the pediment and a carved face on the keystone above the fanlight. Lovely cornice below the shallow parapet. This most elegant facade disguises a very substantial timber-framed house.

Tudor Cottage and Archway Cottage
A few yards further down from Mansel Hall. Two timber-framed and plastered houses. The first with a gabled cross-wing with canted bays beneath and a main hall block alongside but this time jettied which means that it has been two-storied since it was built, c. 1550. Next door is another Hall house with gabled cross-wings. Hall divided horizontally but the original doorway giving access to the Screens' Passage has survived, c. 1500.

Corpus Christi or Cadge's House
An important late fifteenth century building of great interest. What appears to be three cottages with early nineteenth century windows and doors and a long facade completely rough-cast disguises what is believed to be the Hall of the Guild of Corpus Christi. I have not been able to substantiate the claim but certainly the internal features point to a hall of that type. In its original form it consisted of a great hall with cross-wings at either side, all of which can be deduced from the roof levels as usual. Internal evidence shows that the upper floors of the wings were jettied and the carved

bressumers which supported the projecting superstructure are still in position behind the later facade. Because they are carved we know that the timber frame was meant to be exposed. The central hall, which apparently was not jettied and has been horizontally divided at a later date, has a crown post roof. Throughout the timbers are exceptionally sturdy and there are several original arched doorways, some of them blocked.

The upper room of the northern cross-wing is of special interest because of its ceiling and fragmented wall painting. The roof is a low-pitched cambered tie-beam construction, similar to the Lady Chapel in the church and of the same date but in its details quite different. Both ridge beam and all the close set rafters are deeply moulded but the principal tie-beam is merely chamfered. The rafters slope gently to the wall plate which forms a deep and richly carved cornice with variations of a battlemented motif. There is no foliage carving as at Melford Place. At each end of the ridge beam are carved human heads, one of a man with a full moustache and the other of a woman with a plump face, her hair parted at the centre and falling in ringlets. The space between the rafters is boarded.

The studwork of the walls is fully exposed and both timber and plaster bear traces of colour decoration. Much of this is now faded and worn and is difficult to distinguish but appears to be of a later date, probably middle sixteenth century, and is mostly organic. There are considerable remains of a border, about one foot in depth, of fruit. Below that there are several indications of a large pattern of stylised fruit and trees similar to the tapestry designs of that period. In one corner there are two distinct human figures, one standing and the other kneeling, the fragmentary dress details pointing to c. 1560. There is a blocked

Hall Street, East Side: Forge Cottage with 17C plaster over earlier timber frame.

Hall Street, West Side: Georgian bays fronting older cottages. All very typical of Melford and most appealing.

Hall Street, Chapel Green: Medieval chimneys betray the origins of this apparently Victorian house. Possibly incorporating the remains of a tavern.

arched doorway in the north wall which suggests that the cottages alongside may have formed an extension but the plaster infill is also painted.

The wall painting was applied after the suppression of the guilds when this building was converted to domestic use.

Old Forge Cottage Timber-framed, thatched and jettied with a few exposed timbers poking through the thick seventeenth century plaster. The timber frame is older and it would seem that this very attractive cottage is the surviving cross-wing of a much larger dwelling.

Chapel Green It takes its name from the vanished medieval chapel of St. James. A tree marks the approximate site and close by is a very welcome seat where we can rest before making our return journey.

Flanking the north side of the green is a large Victorian house with original Tudor chimney stacks. This may well represent the home of Roger Moryell who kept:— ". . . a tavern in Halle Street on the east side in Melforde near the olde market and held there a piece of the waste land of the manor in front of the tavern gate." It has been suggested that the waste land was acquired for erecting a sign. Chapel Green was indeed the site of the original market granted to Melford by King John. Roger Moryell was a posthumous contributor to the church rebuilding fund through his widow.

Hall Street, West Side

Melford Place Already described but the long red brick garden wall is worth studying. Close by the house is a short section which marks the width of the vanished north wing. Adjoining is a stretch of sixteenth century English bonding followed by a longer stretch of Jacobean Flemish bonding.

There follows a group of four terraces of

nineteenth century flint cottages and several others of various dates and styles until we reach St. Catherine's Road. On the corner is a patisserie which has a medieval timber frame much prettied by the Victorians. Then an attractive timber and plastered group before we come to the old Meeting House, now the United Reformed Chapel.

United Reformed Chapel Red brick, square, with a pair of tall round-headed windows flanking the centre doorway. In the grounds an undulating or serpentine wall and a remarkable tree CATALPA BIGNONIODES or Indian Bean Tree. Inside the chapel is a handsome but simple eighteenth century pulpit with slender balustrade to the steps. All other furnishings Victorian, ceiling renewed and a few tomb slabs from the eighteenth century.

Until this chapel was built in 1712 the early non-conformists met in barns and houses. The nearby Manse appears to be of the same date.

The Gables and Almacks The Gables is a Hall house with cross-wings, refronted and remodelled in the early nineteenth century. A little too sombre for Hall Street, but an original chimney stack still survives. Even more sombre is Almacks which takes its name from the man who rebuilt the house. A broad Victorian front, gabled in a heavy handed Tudor style with ornate barge boards and Gothic doorcase. Another original chimney stack suggests that some of the older house may have survived inside.

The Old House At the time of writing a restaurant. A timber-framed house from the early sixteenth century with all its timbers exposed as they were meant to be in this instance. A good solid structure with a broad front and jettied upper floor. Originally three oriel windows but only two have survived. Ground floor bay windows at either end are Georgian and the original entrance was probably at the centre. A wealth of exposed timber inside and some original fireplaces. A narrow staircase with the treads

Hall Street, West Side: The Old House with exposed timber-frame fronting the street and later seventeenth century extension at the rear with dormers.

Hall Street, West Side: Late Georgian facade c. 1815 to Foundry House on the left and an earlier stuccoed front to the Cock and Bell.

rising in spiral fashion round a central pole shaft. Excellent chimney stack with four massive octagonal shafts. Later extension at the rear with dormers leaning at a crazy angle dates from the early seventeenth century and has great character.

Foundry House and Cock and Bell Inn   With the Old House they form a most attractive group. Foundry House has a four bay white brick facade of c. 1815 with a very shallow parapet. Three-storied and beautifully proportioned with a generous spacing of windows but the ground floor has been spoiled with the insertion of a shop front to the left of the elegant doorcase. The interior is timber-framed. Behind this building was the Iron Foundry of Messrs. Ward and Silver until 1953.

The Cock and Bell is also timber-framed with a late eighteenth century plastered facade. A deep parapet and decorative quoins at the corners. Four broad bays with centre doorcase. Two bays on the left canted, those on the right with hood moulds. A typical homely inn of the period of the type often seen on coaching prints. It has been an inn for over two hundred years and tradition has it that cock fighting was regularly held in the yard.

Hanwell House   A remarkable building, even for Melford. A three bay Georgian red brick facade of c. 1750 fronting a timber-framed dwelling reputed to be a former guildhall. Its most outstanding feature is the surfeit of Venetian windows — four on a relatively narrow front.

The Venetian window was introduced into English architecture during the late seventeenth century and its prime use was to provide an accent or focal point to a facade as well as providing extra light to the interior. To see it used to maximum effect locally one should visit Gosfield Church (open Sunday afternoons only) and see the Wentworth chapel. We have also seen it used most effectively across the road at Mansel Hall. Here at Hanwell House such effectiveness is completely lost through excessive use. It should be pointed out that the centre arch of each window is non-functional and additional windows were inserted at the side but have since been blocked. Paradoxically four such windows on a public building would be acceptable but on a house of this size would expose the owner to some ridicule. We are bound to ask the question whether this building served as an assembly room during the transition from guildhall to house? There is a delicious Adam-type pedimented doorcase and one has to admit that the house has a robust cheekiness which has to be admired.

List House to Cocoa Nut House

A few doors down is the handsome seven bay front with two good pedimented doorcases with panelled reveals. Very late eighteenth century in lovely toned grey brick. A nice run of sashed windows a little irregularly spaced which points to a timber frame behind the facade. The timber construction appears to be of two periods, most of it sixteenth century, the remainder a century later. Behind this house was a horsehair factory in the nineteenth century, one of several such establishments in the village.

There follows a very pleasant run of Georgian facades with an assortment of doorcases, bay windows, etc. each making a quiet contribution to the unquestioned attractiveness of the street. The Victorian Lecture Hall or Working Man's Club in Gothic style is mercifully quiet. It was the centre flashpoint of the Election Riot of 1885. The Swan Inn has a very attractive late Georgian facade of three bays with timber framing behind. The outer bays are canted and the whole front is painted brick, a habit which should be discouraged. Old mellow brickwork is one of the great attractions of Melford; it should be left exposed.

Nearby is a particularly attractive late Georgian shop front with twin shallow canted bay

Hall Street, West Side: Hanwell House with a Georgian facade of c. 1750 fronting a timber-framed building reputed to have been a Guildhall. The four Venetian windows suggest that this may have served as an Assembly Room during the transition from Guildhall to house.

Hall Street, West Side: List House with a late eighteenth century facade with beautiful doorways fronting a timber frame of two periods.

windows, the finest in Melford. Finally we reach Cocoa Nut House, a red brick Victorian front to a gabled timber-framed Hall house. Coconut matting was made here during the late nineteenth century. Immediately in front of the house is the site of the small, medieval covered market and across the road is the Bull Hotel where we started our journey.

WESTGATE STREET

This street is part of the Roman road from Barham to Wixoe and is now the A1092 to Clare which enters Melford at the top of the Green by the church. Immediately joining the Black Lion is a remarkable sight even for a village the size of Melford. A terrace of houses, three-storied in grey brick with slate roofs, obviously a building speculation of c. 1835—8 of the kind one would expect to find in a town such as Bury St. Edmunds or Ipswich. Undeniably attractive and elegant with a nice run of sash windows and simple doorways. The first has a pedimented gable which suggests that additional houses were planned but apparently the builder ran out of funds. In complete contrast a few doors down is a delightful thatched house, timber-framed and plastered, with flint and brick extensions. Recently very carefully restored. On the same side, about one hundred yards further down is Westgate House. Grey brick front with deep eaves board, seven bays wide with a pedimented centre. Handsome pedimented doorcase with a Gibbs surround. All late eighteenth century but parts of the rear are timber-framed and plastered and obviously earlier. Good interior with pillared hall and simple but elegant staircase, ceiling cornices and fireplaces. A splendid introduction to the pleasures of Melford when entering from the west.

BULL LANE AND BRIDGE STREET

Bull Lane is the street which runs alongside the Bull Hotel and about half a mile down is a group of three houses, timber-framed and plastered. One is of the simplest form, originally single storied with a gabled extension. The second is a Hall house of the sixteenth century with gables at either end added

Westgate Street: Early nineteenth century elegance, 1835–38. Remarkably urban for a village.

Westgate Street: Late 16C timber, plastered a century later with flint extensions still later.

Westgate House, 18C elegance again. Note the pedimented doorcase with 'Gibbs' surround, the deep eaves boards and the classic proportions generally.

Bull Lane: Two timber-framed houses on the road to Lavenham

Bull Lane: Another Timber-framed house

Bridge Street Farm: A Hall house with gabled cross-wings, timber-framed and plastered. Splendid array of chimneys.

Bridge Street, Ford Hall: The home of Mary Clopton who married William Cordell of Melford Hall.

a century later and early nineteenth century pillared porch and sash windows. The third often appears on calendars and chocolate boxes because it is very picturesque. Original single storied hall of the early sixteenth century with giant chimney stack inserted later. Slightly later cross-wing with exposed timbers and oversailing, a little tipsy, which adds charm.

Bridge Street is a hamlet to the north of the village on the Bury road and en route can be seen Bridge Street Farm on the left hand side. This is a most attractive timber-framed house, hall and cross-wings with splendid tall chimney shafts. At Bridge Street, a short distance from the road on the right, can be seen Ford Hall, originally Fore Hall, a timber-framed house from the end of the fifteenth century which was a home of the Cloptons. Mary Clopton lived here before she became the wife of William Cordell of Melford Hall.

ACKNOWLEDGEMENTS

Working on Long Melford has been a pleasure throughout and the task was made much easier through the kind cooperation of so many householders. To all those who allowed me access to their homes I am deeply grateful.

Special thanks are due to the following persons whose assistance was invaluable:

Sir Richard Hyde Parker Bt. at Melford Hall.

Mr. Patrick Phillips at Kentwell Hall.

Mr. C. Westropp Cutler at Melford Place.

The assistants at the Record Offices of Bury St. Edmunds, Ipswich and Norwich.

The Librarians at Colchester Reference Library and the Guildhall Library in London.

The Curator of the Sir John Soane's Museum in London.

Special thanks also to Ken Haines whose photographs are an essential part of this book. His endless patience and support are most gratefully appreciated.